Beginning With Chiles

How to Roast, Peel and Prepare
Chile Peppers for
Authentic Mexican Salsas,
Stuffers and Seasonings

Mary Lou Creechan
Jim Creechan

Beginning With Chiles:
How to Roast, Peel and Prepare Chile Peppers for Authentic Mexican Sauces, Stuffers and Seasonings

1999

Mary Lou Creechan
Jim Creechan

ISBN 0-9685066-0-7

Published by Tiengui del Norte Publishing
Box 62, 9920 - 63 Avenue
Edmonton, Alberta T6E 0G9
Canada

(780) 903-0377
email rrrico@globalserve.net

Published in Canada
Printed by Sunrise Printing, Edmonton, Alberta, Canada

Cover Design by Flavio Rojas

Photos by Jim Creechan

Dedicated to our children
Dave and Simone,
and to the memory of
Gordon and Mary Purdy

Preface

We in non tropical climes are just beginning to appreciate what Native Americans have known since 7000 BC— that the rich sophisticated flavours and nutritional value of chile peppers cannot be equaled. Chile peppers are nutritious (a wonderful source of Vitamins A and C, riboflavin, fiber and sodium), flavourful, versatile and fat free. Chile peppers can add a fresh, piquant quality to a salad, a rich earthy flavour to a salsa; they can heat up your favorite condiment, season your meat, fish, stew or soup. They can be stuffed whole, dried and ground, roasted and chopped, smoked and made into sauces.

Surprisingly little has been written about the origins and evolution of this fascinating food. That's beginning to change, and now there are books describing the long history of native and domesticated chiles, the cultural significance for the Aztecs, the Maya and the Tohono O'odham, the medical applications, the nutritional value and even the legends and anecdotes surrounding them are increasingly available. And, on a more scientific level, experts continuously gather production data about the flavours and qualities of new and hybrid varieties.

Mexico is a major producer of chiles, and per person still consumes them most. Because of their lengthy experience with this food, they've developed infinite ways of preparing fresh and dried chiles. Without a doubt, when it comes to chiles, Mexicans rule.

Why 'Beginning with Chiles'?

We've called our book *Beginning with Chiles* because it is for those of you who would like to tap into the exotic, flavourful world of chile peppers *but don't quite know where to begin*. Perhaps you're deterred by the seemingly endless varieties of chiles, their different flavours and heat levels, or perhaps you're just uncertain about their preparation and use. Whatever the reason *Beginning with Chiles* is designed to get you started— with fascinating facts, useful tips and easy start up recipes using the most commonly available chiles.

And yes, there are numerous varieties and sub-varieties of chiles. There's no end to their shapes, sizes, colours, names, heat levels and flavours! And to add to the confusion, the names can change depending on their place of origin. In this book we'll introduce you to this world of chile peppers but we focus primarily on the most common varieties— those readily available in supermarkets and specialty stores. And we organize these common varieties (like the jalapeño, serrano, poblano) by how they are most often used. Hence our chapters are titled "the Snappies", "the Stuffers", "the Smoothies" and "Seasoners".

We've also selected recipes that will help familiarize you with these chiles and get you started with some simple preparations. Once you know the basics, you can go wild and create your own masterpieces. Or, you can check out some of the excellent Mexican and southwest cookbooks that we've recommended.

Why us?

When we first became interested in chile peppers, we looked for a cook book that would provide general information about the most common chiles, basic descriptions of their characteristics, and some simple tips about preparation. We also tried to find a collection of straightforward recipes which would highlight the flavour of chiles, use widely available ingredients, and which would be easy to use. In other words, we were looking for a book like Beginning with Chiles. It would have made our introduction to the chile experience a whole lot smoother. We hope our book will do that for you.

As chiles become more widely available north of the Rio Grande, friends and acquaintances often ask us *which chiles to buy* and *how to prepare them*. They want a *general* understanding of how to use them in recipes, and they want to know what flavours and textures they add. In this book we answer those basic questions, keeping in mind the historical traditions and cultural context from which they come. Hopefully, our personal anecdotes and informational notes give you an appreciation of how much this food and culture are intertwined.

Chile peppers are such an integral part of our personal daily diet we can't imagine a world without them. We've been reading and working with chiles for many years and yet we continue to unearth fascinating facts about this exotic food. It's always possible to do something wonderful with a chile— whether it's a simple salsa or a complex mole. And despite the availability of more sophisticated kitchen utensils, the basic preparation techniques are unchanged.

Chiles are exotic and exciting, much like the culture from which they come. They've been apart of our world for many years. We hope Beginning with Chiles will make them a part of yours.

Mary Lou and Jim Creechan
Toronto, Ontario and Edmonton, Alberta
March 1999

Our Personal World of Chile Peppers

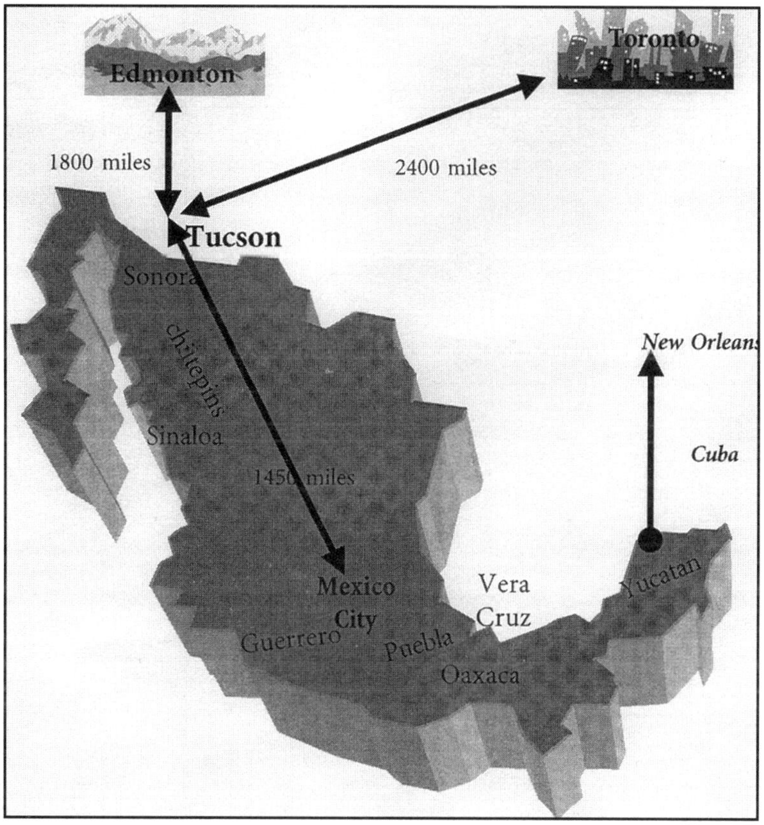

Our world of chiles covers all three NAFTA countries. We began with chiles in Tucson, Arizona, struggled to find them in Edmonton, Alberta and Toronto, Ontario and learned lots more about them in Los Angeles, California and Mexico City, Mexico. Now the most common varieties of chiles are available in many locations making your world of chiles a whole lot easier, we hope.

How We Began with Chiles

By Mary Lou Creechan

It all started long ago when my family (for medical reasons) found it necessary to spend the better part of each year in Tucson, Arizona— a long 2400 mile drive from our Toronto home. In Tucson, we were introduced to a new country, a new culture, and most importantly (for me)— a new cuisine. I say 'for me' because...well, you know the old saying— "some people eat to live, others live to eat".

Needless to say in Tucson my culinary world exploded— *chile verde, barbacoa, machaca, green corn tamales*— the food was flavourful, rich, and exotic! And I (along with my family) was hooked!

The food became part of my luggage. I hauled it back to Toronto— beginning with the simple stuff— canned chiles, enchilada sauce, and dried pinto beans. Later on, the perishables— *flour tortillas, queso fresco*, and fresh *Anaheim chiles.* I became a pioneer in travelling with food— by car, by train, by rail and even more challenging— through customs.

Everything went well until the trips stopped— unfortunately in Toronto. For the next few years I went without, or survived on meager, pricey imports. Then I met Jim and got married. At the time, Jim was cautiously contemplating a graduate degree, weighing the pros and cons of various graduate schools. Now I don't for one minute suggest that he chose the University of Arizona because of my need for *chile rellenos* and *green corn tamales*—but...

There I was back at the source, gradually introducing Jim and then our two children to *albondigas, machacas, flautas, chile verde*, and *tostadas*— and to favorite restaurants like El Minuto, Mi Nidito, El Charro, La Fuente and El Dorado. Up to this point I was quite content with restaurant food or my own primitive efforts prepared with bottled salsas, canned beans and chiles and packaged tortillas. Not Jim! He approached this new cuisine with the cool objectivity of a scientist. He researched, analyzed, tested, and, with the help of Mexican friends, learned the 'real' way. Our culinary needs graduated to fresh chiles and salsas, homemade tortillas and tamales, sun dried machaca, hand ground and freshly seasoned *chorizo*.

Then we moved to Edmonton, Alberta Canada. Our last Mexican meal was in Medford, Oregon. Now don't get me wrong. Edmonton is a remarkably cosmopolitan place. There was even ...uh... a "Mexican" restaurant. One bright note was a now defunct yet at the time visionary chain of stores in Alberta called Woodwards. They actually carried "foreign food" which for us meant canned whole green chiles, refried beans and a few salsas. So with their help, regular trips to Tucson, and visits from my family we made do.

One year we managed a sabbatical in the southwest where our interest in Mexican food intensified. We discovered the cuisine of southern Mexico— *moles, pipians,* and *adobos*. We discovered dried chiles, blue corn, and *pozole*. Our luggage now included such odd items as cornhusks, blue corn flour, and a weed called *epazote*. Meanwhile others around us were beginning to "discover" southwestern and Mexican food.

In Edmonton, we hooked up with a group of academics who shared our passion. This led to new dishes and recipes. And Jim's cooking expertise grew as fresh products and wonderfully informative cookbooks became available. Even I, normally motivated by more primal urges, delved into the complicated techniques of preparation.

Then came Chile Pepper Magazine and '*the contest*'. Of course Jim entered a recipe so complex that I truly believe that they gave him the prize to avoid its preparation. He won *Best of Show* for his original Heritage Harvest Blue Corn Bread,— a feat that fostered considerable publicity across the country. Imagine, a Canadian winning a chile pepper contest! This led to requests for recipes, samples, etc. Jim milked it for all it was worth because it was a lot of fun and gave him a prestige not normally accorded to academics.

Besides, our interest in Mexican food has always involved a certain evangelical zeal. We want others to believe! We crusade with banquet size meals for friends and colleagues, with gifts of pickled chiles, and salsas, with the "Baby T"— an original southwestern concoction that we serve at chile festivals. And now, to continue our mission we've written this book which we hope will result in your chile conversion. And just think, you don't have to send them, pack them, or declare them. They're everywhere!

Now if only we could get our hands on some decent tortillas!

Photo Courtesy of the University of Alberta New Trail Magazine

About the Authors

Mary Lou Creechan was born in Hamilton, Ontario and lived with her family for many years in Tucson, Arizona before she met Jim. Coincidently, he was also born in Hamilton. After marrying in Toronto, Ontario they both enrolled in graduate studies at the University of Arizona in Tucson. It was there that Mary Lou and her family introduced Jim to Sonoran style Mexican-American food and created his lifelong addiction to it.

Over the years, both authors traveled widely in Mexico and the American southwest, and were fortunate to live for periods of time in Mexico City, Los Angeles, California and also Tucson, Arizona. The luxury of an academic job provided the opportunity for sabbaticals in these incredibly interesting cities.

During their marriage, they have always cooked Mexican food and gathered exotic collections of Mexican spices and ingredients. At the University of Alberta in Edmonton, they were the occasional organizers of an annual pot-luck fiesta which featured Mexican recipes. Unfortunately, this was so succesful that it outgrew everybody's party space and is now just a fond memory.

Mary Lou Creechan is a broadcaster, writer and restaurateur. She reviewed restaurants for CBC Edmonton radio, and authored a best-selling book on Edmonton restaurants (Best of Edmonton). She hosted a jazz show (Mid-Morning) and a Latin music show (The Latin Quarter) for the Access Radio Network - CKUA in Alberta. Currently, she is hosting a jazz and Latin jazz show (Night Beat) on Toronto's CJRT-FM. She is the co-owner with her sister, Kris Purdy, of a catering business ***¡ RRRico by Night !*** in Toronto, Ontario.

Jim Creechan is a professor of sociology and a criminologist at the University of Alberta. More than 11,000 students have taken his classes and he hopes many of them will buy this book. His recipe for Blue Corn Bread won the ***Best of Show Prize*** in the 1994 Chile Pepper Magazine Cooking Contest. This led to a minor flurry of fame because people weren't sure how a Canadian won this contest. His interest in Mexican food began in the 1960's when he lived in Mexico City and visited some remote parts of the Sierra Huasteca. He is an avid collector of cookbooks, and has grown some strange and exotic Mexican ingredients in the family garden. Strains of epazote mysteriously appearing in the Canadian prairies probably originated in his garden.

Table of Contents

Fresh Chiles

Dried Chiles

Recipes

Jalapeños

Serranos

Habaneros

Stuffer recipes.

Smoothie Recipes

Seasoner Recipes

Chipotle Recipes

Using This Book

This book focuses on commonly available chiles which we've organized by use. Hence the rather unusual titles of *Snappies for Salsas*, *The Stuffers*, *The Smoothies*, and *Seasoners*. Smaller chiles are generally used for *salsas*, larger ones for *stuffers*, dried ones for *smooth salsas*. We thought these titles would make it easier to remember the various types, their use, and also encourage you to substitute if you can't find the exact chile specified in a recipe.

We've divided the book into two major sections. The first section deals with ***fresh chile peppers*** and the second with ***dried chile peppers***. Each section contains a general introduction to the most common chiles in that category followed by a detailed description of each and some typical recipes. We've also included notes of interest, cooking tips, historical anecdotes and various tidbits that we've gathered travelling in the Southwest and Mexico, reading about chile peppers and, of course from our love of cooking and eating them.

For those of you who want more information, we've included chile charts, a list of recommended books, festivals and internet sites and a few extra thoughts at the end of the book.

But first and foremost *Beginning with Chiles* is an introduction to the exotic world of chiles. Here's hoping it's your ticket to many sensational, chile adventures.

Buen Provecho!

Formatting and information on presentation style

The main narrative of this book is written in the same textface used in this paragraph. This textface describes the basic information about the various chiles.

Besides the main narrative, we've included other information in our book. A distinct textface is used to describe this additional information. We also decided to use special *icons* to help you recognize the type of information.

Chile Tips

This symbol is used to indicate a ***Special Tip*** about chile handling and and preparation. These are also enclosed in a special text box.

Mexico Map

This symbol indicates a story about ***Mexican history, geography, vocabulary, or custom***. It is also enclosed in a special text box.

Glossary Symbol

This symbol indicates that a ***word or term is being explained or defined***. It is also in a special textbox at the bottom of a page.

In the recipe sections, we have also used two additional symbols.

Shopping List

The shopping cart and bags indicates the ***ingredients*** necessary for a recipe.

Preparation Technique

A chef in a kitchen is located beside the ***instructions for assembly and preparation.***

History, Heat and Handling

Chile Peppers have been around for thousands of years- yet in many areas of North America they're just now becoming widely available.
Where did they originate?
How many varieties are there?
Are they all hot?

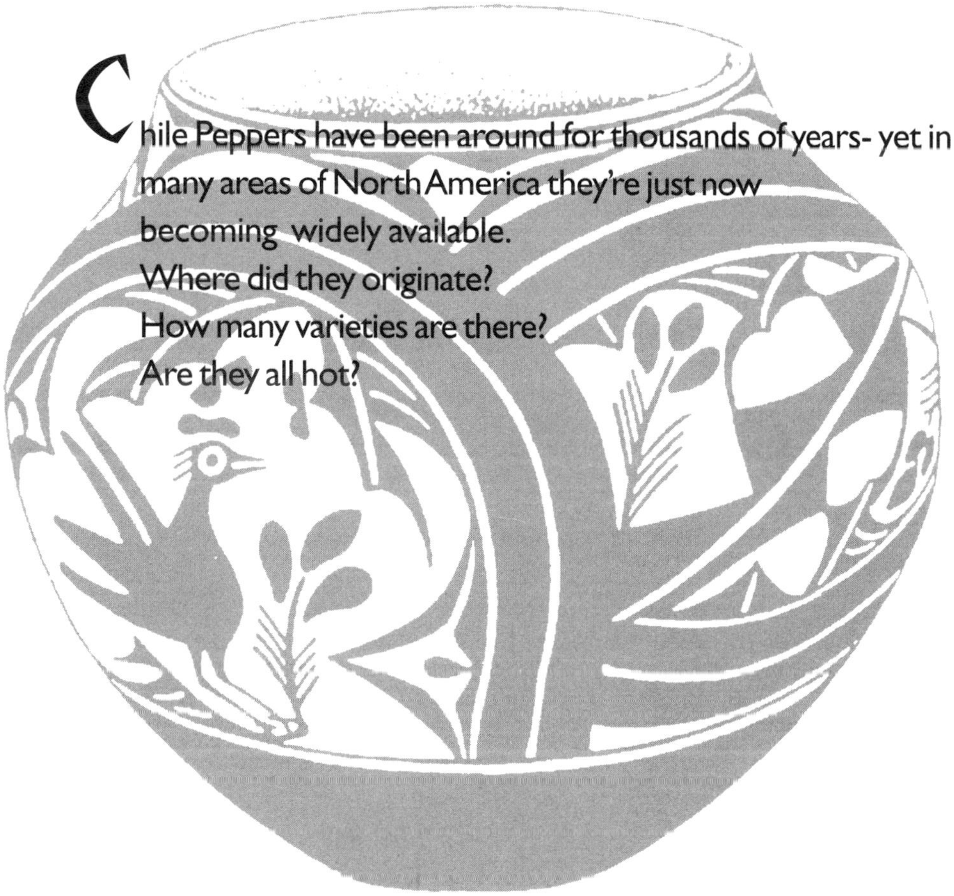

Was there a *chile numero uno*?

There may have been several. Botanists now tell us that wild chiles were domesticated at least 5 times on the North and South American continents— but the biggest number and widest variety of chiles are all part of one group originally domesticated in Mexico. This single family comes from central Mexico and includes almost all of the chiles we routinely find at the market today. These are the ones that we'll concentrate on in this book.

Now back to the original question! Was there a numero uno? *Yes* say the experts— this ancestral family of most North American chiles does have a *numero uno.* It first appeared thousands of years ago in a semi arid region in the north and resembles the small *chiltepin* that still grows wild in the Sonoran desert of Mexico and the United States. They also say that migrant birds, apparently the first chileheads, were attracted to these bright tiny berries, gobbled them up and then spread the seeds across a wide area west of the Sierra Madre Oriental.

We'll never know the name of the chef who first seasoned a meal with this picante bird seed— but, we do know that several nomadic peoples gathered berries and carried seeds along southwestern routes of North America, down the west coast of Mexico and back north into parts of modern day Arizona and California. And later on, when more permanent settlements were established, these prized chiles were domesticated alongside other important foods like corn (*maiz*), squash and beans.

Tenochtitlan: capital of the Aztec Empire, founded about 1325. It had about 200,000 residents when Hernán Cortés arrived in 1519.

Tlatelolco: An important ceremonial center and market north of Tenochtitlan which was joined by a major causeway across the lake. Its market had as many as 25,000 merchants.

But the discovery of a wild version was just the beginning of the chile adventure. Those early pre-Hispanic farmers began to select and develop chiles for their flavours and shapes, and they learned to use them to complement basic foods like corn, squash, beans and tomatoes. In their earliest experiments, these tribes gave birth to chiles of many colours, shapes, sizes, tastes, textures and heat levels.

And if that wasn't enough of a contribution— they also developed methods of preserving and drying chiles so they could be enjoyed all year round.

The modern day site of the market at Tlatelolco in Mexico City.
Fray Bernardo de Sahagún wrote the General History of New Spain here!

Many centuries later, the Aztecs were cultivating, consuming and marketing an incredible variety of domesticated chiles. They transported them from nearby floating gardens (*chinampas*) and from even more distant places to be sold in the large markets of Tenochtitlan and Tlatelolco. Many of the Aztec trade routes wove their way through chile country—from Xalapa, Vera Cruz (home of the famous jalapeño), through Tlaxcala, and then through Cholula and Huejotzingo (near modern day Puebla)— and then on to the giant markets in Tlatelolco. According to Spanish chroniclers the variety of chiles sold at these Aztec markets was tremendous! Some writers described with amazement the existing classification system for chiles, and they couldn't resist including recipes for a variety of salsas.

"They eat many types of 'vegetable mixtures with chiles'; one was made with a yellow chile, another of a chile mixture made of chopped chiles and tomatoes, and another chile mixture made of yellow chile and tomato"

Fray Bernardo de Sahagún,
Historia General de Los Cosas de Nueva España,
Libro Octavo, 1566-1571

Unfortunately for the Aztecs, those same trade routes brought Hernán Cortés, Pedro de Alvarado and many others to that marvelous city on the central plateau. Those early conquistadores were hungry— but their appetite wasn't for the wondrous new foods that grew along the routes. As Cortés told Montezuma's messengers, Castillians had a "*hunger which only gold could cure*".

These early plunderers were preoccupied with melting down many magnificent legacies of the pre-Hispanic world and destroying cities in search of more. But, eventually their Castillian food sources ran out and they had to eat foods which they found along the way, and which Indian women taught them to use. Thankfully, as gourmands, they came to appreciate this food and in particular the rich and exotic chile.

The first Spanish settlements were in Hispaniola and Cuba (1493). But when the Europeans saw a potential for wealth further to the west there was a frantic rush across the Gulf of Mexico. Hernan Cortés was an adventurer who landed in the Yucatan in 1519 and began hearing rumours about the Aztec empire. At one stop, he was presented with 20 Indian women as 'gifts'. These women introduced the Castillians to the local foods which they learned to blend with the remaining supplies from the Caribbean islands.

Now that we know a little bit about how it all began, let's begin our own exploration of the chile peppers from Mexico. But, first a salute to the good taste and imagination of all who came before— the Chichimeca, the Aztecs, the Maya, the O' odham, and even the Castillian adventurers. Most importantly, let us toast the Mexicans of today who have sustained and enhanced this culinary legacy for all of us to enjoy.

"Let us worship the chile with the highest form of merit,
a tribute to its trail of adventures
from our pre-Hispanic kitchens
to the universal table"

(homage to chile by the poet Salvador Novo)

The word chile is spelled in different ways. The original is an Aztec (*Nahuatl)* word 'chilli'.

Mexicans spell it with an 'e' (chile). In England it contains a double 'll' and ends in'i'. It is also spelled' chili.

It is all the same thing– but we prefer the Spanish spelling– "chile".

Botanists now recognize 5 members of the chile family

Capsicum: The general Genus name for all chiles. There are 22 wild species (e.g. the chiltepin), and 5 domesticated species:

• *Capsicum* **annum**: By far the largest of the 5 species. With three exceptions, every domestic chile we buy in the supermarket is a member of this species. These are the chiles found in Mexico and the American Southwest.

• *Capsicum* **frutescens**: the famous Tabasco chile, now associated with Louisiana is a member of this species. An American soldier who was part of Vera Cruz invasion of the late 1840's brought it to Louisiana and gave it to the McIlhenny family.

• *Capsicum* **chinense**: The unique scotch bonnet and habanero are members of this species. It is associated with the Caribbean and the Yucatan.

• *Capsicum* **baccatum**: This is the common chile species from South America. It is called '*aji*' and not chile. The term probably came from a Caribbean tribe (the Arawak) who named them '*agi*'.

• *Capsicum* **pubescens**: This is a relatively rare chile in North America. The most distinct characteristic is black seeds. It is found from southern Mexico to Peru, and often has an apple or pear shape.

Pequins: only about 1/8" wide, these are a close relative of the wild chiltepin.

In South American countries chiles are usually called aji. 'Agi' was the name used by Arawak and Carib Indians for a chile pepper found in the Caribbean. Conquistadors based in Hispaniola and Cuba took the name 'aji' to South America. On the other hand, conquistadors who went to Mexico adopted the many chile names already in use there.

Also, chiles from the Caribbean were brought to Europe before 1500. These chiles were mistakenly thought to be related to the black pepper, thus creating another source of name confusion. Chile peppers are not related to black table pepper.

Not long ago when many of us heard the word *chili* we thought of that Tex-Mex concoction of meat, beans, tomatoes and exotic spices. We thought of chile cookoffs, fiery food fairs and hotter than hell salsas. Lately though, with increased travel to the Southwest, Mexico, South America and the Caribbean we've managed to move beyond this rather narrow characterization of the chile to appreciate its versatility and wide range of flavours.

Many of us have sampled the red and green chile sauces of New Mexico, the spicy meat mixtures of Arizona, the chile rellenos of Southern California and the salsas and moles of Mexico. These chile based foods are now being served throughout North America, and many varieties of chiles are available. Soon, chiles will become as common as sun dried tomatoes and balsamic vinegar.

Chiles fit into several food categories. They may be referred to as a vegetable, spice, fruit or berry.

Leave this name debate to the botanists, chemists, and nutritionists.

Fresh chiles are vegetables and *dried* chiles are spices.

Mole is the ultimate in chile cuisine, combining the flavours of many different types of chiles– especially pasillas, anchos and mulatos. One famous dish– **enchiladas tres moles**– uses mole poblano, green pipian (a type of mole) and red pipian. It's as flavourful as it is colourful! And once you've had it, you'll crave it forever.

They're easy to use!

Fresh or dried— chiles are actually prepared in simple ways. They're *toasted, peeled* and *stuffed*, or they are *crushed* and mixed with a *liquid* or dry ingredients. It's as straightforward as that! Some of the most flavourful chile dishes are very *simple* combinations of prepared chiles mixed with a few other ingredients.

In *Tamaulipas Mexico* evidence of the chile in human diets was discovered at several sites at least 8,000 years old.

Many wonderful chile dishes have been around for centuries. And despite the arrival of sophisticated time savers like food processors or spice grinders, the basic preparation remains unchanged. *Pico de Gallo*, one of Mexico's most familiar salsas, is a simple mixture of serrano chiles, tomatoes, onion and cilantro. And yet, this simple salsa adds a world of flavour to almost any dish.

Of course some of the most classic dishes of Mexico are more demanding. Remember the elaborate preparation of meals in the movie *Like Water for Chocolate*? Those incredible *Chiles en Nogada* require a major commitment. So do those wonderfully rich *moles*— mixtures of chiles, nuts, spices, fruits, vegetables, and seasonings which are cooked for hours. As you become familiar with basic preparation techniques, perhaps you'll want to use chiles in these more complicated dishes; perhaps you'll be creating your own *pipians, recados*, or *adobos*. But, let's start with the basics!

Many botanists think that an *ancestral* chile emerged somewhere in modern day Bolivia. They think that birds spread seeds northwards and several botanical families eventually emerged. Most of the chiles in our book are descendants of families that emerged in the north of Mexico.

Are all chiles hot?

All chiles do have some degree of heat, or what is called the *picante* quality. While many are very hot— even dangerous, other chiles are moderate or mild and are appreciated for their subtle flavours. There are many books that provide complicated classification scales indicating degree of heat.

While it's not really necessary to know technical information such as a chile's *Scoville* number in order to use it in cooking for purposes of eating and handling it is a good idea to become generally acquainted with heat levels.

Most of the widely available chiles we'll use fall below the median level on all heat scales, and they should be tolerable to all but the unadventurous.

Foods and mixtures which contain chiles

salsa: a mixture of chopped ingredients, usually containing a chile.
enchilada: a corn tortilla, filled with cheese or meat and smothered in a smooth sauce made of rehydrated dried chiles.
mole: a more complex mixture of many chiles, fruits, nuts and vegetables.
purée: a smooth mixture of an ingredient which has been crushed or processed.
pipian: a mixture of spices and nuts, almost always containing pumpkin seed .
recado: a dry mixture of spices and chiles; sometimes mixed with bitter orange.
adobo: a mixture of dried spices and chiles usually mixed with a vinegar.

We prefer to use chiles more for their flavour than for their heat. In fact, when chiles are too hot their distinctive flavour is often lost on our palate. The secret is to keep spiciness to a manageable level so that any chile's complex flavour is appreciated. Most chile recipes call for deveining and deseeding and this always lessens the heat level.

In the tropics, hot chiles can actually cool you off– like a mini air conditioner that works from the inside out. You eat, you sweat, and then cool down.

Hot Chile Facts:

- **Generally, the *smaller* the chile the *hotter.***
- ***Dried* chiles are hotter than their *fresh* version.**
- **Fat, fleshy chiles pack more heat after they are smoked or pickled.**
- **Colour is *not* an indication of heat level.**
- **Fresh chiles *lose* a little heat when cooked.**
- **Dried chiles *gain* a little heat when cooked.**

How hot are they?

Two scales measure heat:

The Chile Heat Scale ranks chile heat from 1 to 10, much like the Richter Scale for earthquakes. It is logarithmic, so 2 is 10 times hotter than 1 and 10 is 10,000 time hotter. On this scale, a *bell pepper* is a 1 and a *jalapeño* is a 5.

The **Scoville Scale** assigns big numbers to rate the heat. A *bell pepper* is 100 and a *jalapeño* is 5,000. The number refers to the amount of sugar necessary to neutralize the bite.

The hottest? In the fresh category the *habañero* tops both scales—10 on the Chile Heat Scale and more than 100,000 on the Scoville. But dried chiles like the *satanka* from Asia or the *chiltepin* from Sonora, Mexico are considered the hottest.

By the way, these heat scales rely on special tasters to rate the chiles. No chemical test adequately determines the level of heat so real people must do it. Not a job for the faint of tongue! They apparently have very long coffee breaks to allow tastebuds to recover. Very expensive electronic instruments are under development by agribusiness and will eventually use a new scale called an ASTA measure.

Picante: the Spanish term, which is generally used to refer to the 'bite' of a chile. Sometimes the word 'pungent' is used for this characteristic.

Are they too hot to handle?

Chile flesh is not necessarily hot. Heat comes from the oily capsaicin in the veins and membrane.

Seeds and flesh can become hot when this substance is released.

You can develop a tolerance to the heat in chiles, gradually craving hotter and hotter varieties.

No! Chiles are not hot to the *touch*—but they might irritate eyes and sensitive skin if precautions are not taken. When working with chiles, even the mild ones, follow the handling tips which we provide on the next page and you'll avoid the pain of a severe chile burn. Keep in mind that the heat is not confined to the seeds.

A natural ingredient called *capsaicin* creates the *bite* (also called *pungency*) in chiles. Capsaicin is actually concentrated in the white membrane (the placental wall) and it often passes into the flesh or to the seeds. From the flesh it spreads easily to the natural oils on hands and from there it can spread to...*well, almost anywhere*. You've heard the old saying, "*you never know where those hands have been*". Well, if they've been with chiles you'll know where they were.

In the language of most Sonoran desert tribes, the term chile is 'kokoli'. This word is related to their verb 'to hurt'.

Our daughter learned this lesson the hard way. While stocking produce at her supermarket job, she handled some habaneros and, without thinking, wiped sweat from her face. Sure enough the heat from the habanero came in contact with the delicate membrane of her eyelids swelling them shut. No permanent damage but a painful lesson in handling chiles. In the Southwestern USA, hospital emergency rooms often treat such burns— but we have yet to see this injury featured on ER.

Can you enjoy the flavour without the sting?

If you want to take some of the sting out of the hotter chiles like habaneros or jalapeños there are a few ways to do it. First of all, removing the seeds and veins always reduces the heat. But if this is not enough for you, you can also soak the chiles in a light salty liquid or in a buttermilk bath for about 15 minutes. If you use a salt solution, be sure to thoroughly rinse the chiles before using them. You can drink a bit of cream, milk or take a spoonful of honey or peanut butter if your mouth is hot *after* you eat chiles.

Chiles are somewhat unique in the food world. The wild 'version' is prized and valued as much as domesticated ones (the *cultivars*) .

Domesticated chiles are 'pendant' and hang down. Wild chiles attract birds because they are erect and turn red quickly.

Pequins

In the Southwestern U.S. and in Northern Mexico, long time chile aficionados carry their own pouches of small chiles with them. They're close at hand to season food or to clear out the sinuses– much like snuff. Try carrying around your own little pouch of these chiles. Crush and sprinkle over just about any dish. They'll add lots of heat and flavour. But don't forget to wash your hands before you rub your eyes, or go to the bathroom.

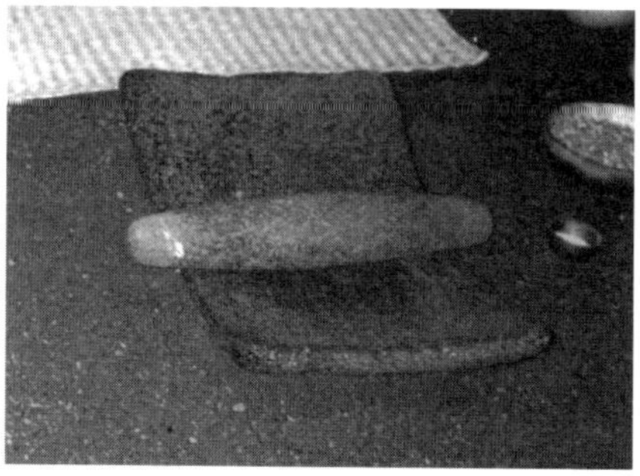

A traditional metate: used for rolling tortillas

Handling Tips:

- Always wash your hands with soap and water before and after using chiles.
- Coat your hands with a light layer of oil or cooking spray before handling chiles (the oil will absorb capsaicin making it easier to wash off).
- Never touch sensitive body parts while working with chiles.
- If you're particularly sensitive to capsaicin, wear latex gloves.
- Remove your rings, because any seeds or veins trapped underneath will burn.
- Squeeze some lime juice on your fingers after handing chiles.
- Try rubbing your fingers through your hair *after* you work with chiles.
- You can also wash your fingers in a mixture of 1 part chlorine bleach and 4 parts water.

The Ruins at Zempoala, Vera Cruz
Hernan Cortés received the first emissaries from Moctezuma at this spot.

The coffee house in the plaza of Coatepec, Vera Cruz
Cortés passed near this spot in 1519 on his way to Mexico City.

BEGINNING WITH

Chiles

FRESH CHILES

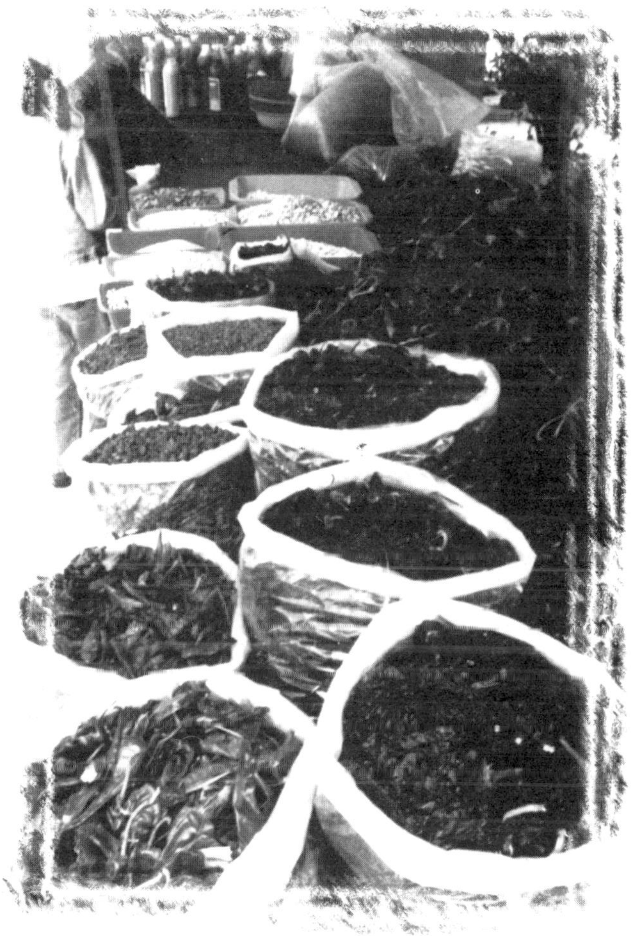

Roasting, Peeling, and Preparing

Fresh chiles are the brightly coloured ones you see everyday in the produce section of your neighborhood market. Jalapeños, serranos, habaneros, poblanos, New Mexico chiles and Anaheims are now widely available. When selecting fresh chiles, choose those which are uniform in colour. The surface should be smooth and shiny with no scaly, brown marks. Avoid those with soft, gray areas and cracks or breaks in the surface. Once you've purchased fresh chiles, store them loosely covered in the fridge until ready to use.

In this chapter we'll describe how to prepare fresh chiles for use. Most chiles are roasted, peeled, deseeded, and deveined. Smaller chiles like serranos and habaneros are exceptions to this rule.

*For hundreds of years the indigenous peoples of the Americas have roasted chiles. They preferred specific types of wood that added flavour– much as we do today on our barbecues. In Mexico the **comal** is most often used for roasting. These are cooking plates of clay or metal and they're available in many sizes to fit over gas or electric burners. Substitute a cast iron pan if you have one.*

Roasting chiles

There's a practical reason to roast— it removes a tough outer skin from larger chiles like poblanos and New Mexico chiles. But there's also a secondary pleasure! Roasting is a unique and *sensual* experience. It produces a fragrance that's earthy, warm and seductive— and it adds a flavour that's rich, complex and satisfying to the chile. So even though it's not necessary for smaller salsa chiles— like the serrano and habanero— *we recommend roasting most chiles*. You *will* taste the difference!

Roasting on the barbecue

A hot barbecue grill is our favorite method of roasting. And, it doesn't really matter whether the heat source is propane, natural gas, hot coals from special woods (mesquite, hickory) or the old standby charcoal. Thoroughly clean the grill with a wire brush and make sure that it is very hot before putting chiles on the grill. Use tongs and turn the chiles frequently to avoid uneven cooking of the flesh.

Anaheims on the barbecue

Remove the chile when the skin has charred slightly and before the chile has completely blackened. Drop into a bag to let the chile "sweat" and to separate the outer skin from the delicious flesh.

Roasting over Direct Gas Flame

If you have a gas stove, use tongs to place a chile directly over the flame. This one-at-a-time method is ideal for preparing a few large chiles for stuffing. However, it's easy to overcook with this method— so turn the chile often. Drop it in a bag to sweat after it is charred.

Chiles are roasted in many different ways.

But no matter how it's done, they are usually dropped into a bag to sweat for a short period of time before further processing.

Direct Flame Roasting of Poblanos

Pan Roasting

If you want to roast a few small chiles, roasting in a frypan is the ideal way. Small chiles fall through cracks of a grill, so pan-frying is a better method. Whenever possible, use a well-seasoned cast iron pan since it produces incomparable results. Roast chiles on a hot dry pan— or for variation, add a small amount of oil to the pan. If you have thick-skinned chiles, then hot oil makes peeling a lot easier. If you're avoiding fat, just slap them on a hot skillet no matter how thick the skin. It's necessary to drop then in a bag to let them sweat even when they are roasted in oil.

Pan roasting Anaheim chiles

Roasting in a Toaster Oven

This really is a great way to roast— especially in counter-top ovens. Turn the broiler element to high heat (above 450°F) and place chiles close to the element without touching. But, *keep a close watch*, because chiles will brown quickly and require frequent turning. Once roasted, follow same bagging procedure used in any method of roasting. (We'll describe this in more detail below).

Roasting time

Roasting time is determined by the toughness of the outer skin. When a chile is fresh from the field (*not much chance*) the skin is very thin and easily removed. However, supermarket chiles have thicker skins allowing for weeks in a warehouse. The outer skin is a bit more stubborn and difficult to remove.

After a few times roasting, you'll learn how to tell when a chile is ready by appearance and even smell. Chiles change colour when heated, and this indicates when they're done. For example, Anaheim chiles change from a bright shiny green to a flat mossy green, and the poblano chile's fresh deep forest-green shine loses its gloss. With a little practice, you'll know that a chile is done by this change in colour.

We think it is better to *slightly undercook* than to overcook— so remove chiles early if you aren't sure. Under-roasted chiles are a little harder to peel, but you can compensate by leaving them to sweat in the bag a little longer. If the outer skin doesn't easily come off on the first one you try to peel, then leave the others in the bag for a longer time.

Sometimes, it's easier to remove skin from a whole chile after it's been frozen.

Try roasting chiles and *freezing* them before peeling. You should find that the skin comes off quite easily when the chile is partially thawed.

In fact, when recipes require *whole* chiles, a slightly frozen one is sometimes easier to clean and prepare.

Anaheim chile ready for the roasting bag

Peeling Chiles

It isn't necessary to peel small chiles like serranos and habaneros. In fact, we recommend you don't! But many others like poblanos, Anaheims and large jalapeños have thick skins that should be removed before they're used. After a chile is roasted (using any of the techniques described above) drop it into a thick plastic bag or a brown paper bag and tightly close it. Let chiles sweat for about 15 to 20 minutes. Remove one from the bag and peel off the skin. By the way, be prepared for a wonderful aroma to saturate the air when you open the bag. The skin almost falls off when a chile is roasted long enough.

Or, you can simply put the chiles in a bowl, cover them with a clear kitchen wrap and allow them to sit for 10-15 minutes to sweat and cool.

Occasionally, we put a brown paper bag inside a thick plastic bag to make a 'special sauna' for roasted chiles. But, keep in mind that fresh roasted chiles are very hot and can melt through a thin container or stick to kitchen-wrap. Sometimes, we even use high quality coffee bags for the sweating period after roasting. These types of bags are moisture resistant and add a *hint* of coffee flavour to the roasted chile.

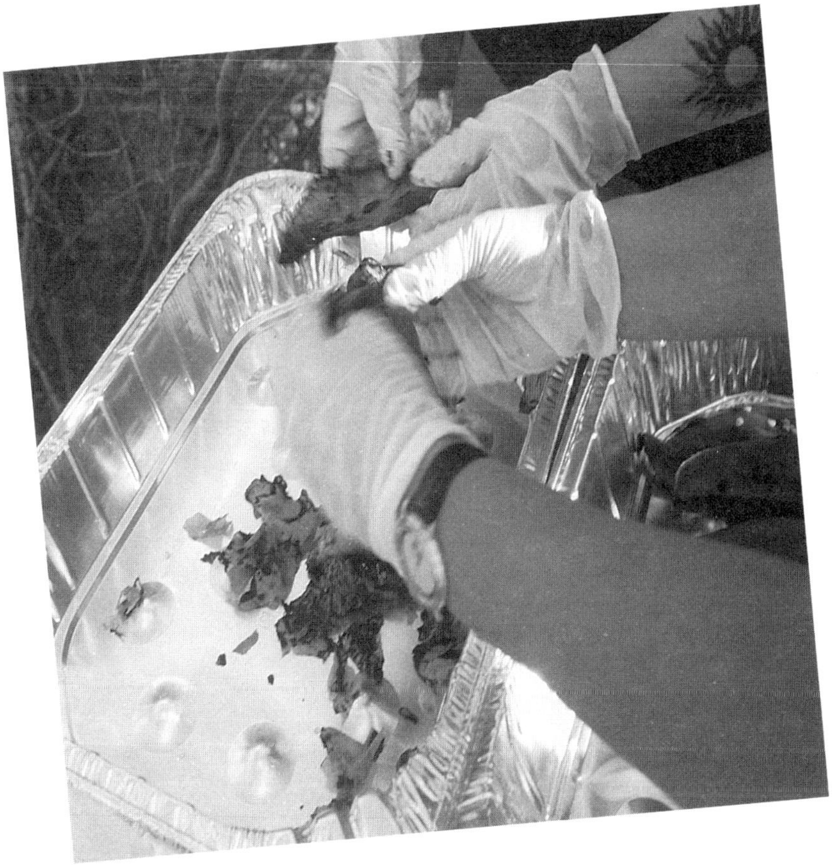

The fresher the chile, the easier to peel. In fact freshly picked chiles can be roasted, dropped in ice water and peeled immediately by simply sliding the chile through a lightly closed fist.

Deseeding and deveining

Removing the seeds and veins reduces the *picante* level of a chile. To remove seeds and veins, use a sharp paring knife with a flexible blade to make a small slit near the top of the chile. Run the paring knife around the inside of the chile to loosen the veins and seeds—making sure to scrape the top where the stem enters the flesh. There is no need to scrape too hard— and in fact too much tasty flesh is removed by pressing too hard. The choicest part is the soft interior flesh, so don't scrape too much. After scraping, pass under a mild stream of cool water to rinse out any remaining seeds and veins and wash away traces of roasted skin. Place them on a paper towel to dry.

As mentioned earlier, the serrano does not need to be deseeded and deveined. Much of the flavour and charm of the serrano is in the seeds. Take them out and you remove the *soul* of this chile.

The process of deveining can be a bit tricky and it definitely takes practice. Don't despair, because every chile is usable— but a *perfectly* cleaned chile looks neater and more pleasing, especially when used for stuffing. Many of our early attempts at cleaning chiles for stuffing were less than successful but this didn't detract from the taste. After deveining and deseeding, your chiles are ready to chop, slice, stuff or store.

Preparing for use in recipes

Chopping

Chop the roasted chiles by hand with a very sharp kitchen knife, or use the chop setting of a food processor. Be careful not to liquefy the flesh if you use a processor— you aren't making a purée. Use a pulsing action by turning on and off in bursts. Place the chopped chiles in a bowl with the oils and juices that are produced by chopping. Make the chile pieces larger for more distinct flavours, or smaller to create a fusion of tastes.

Slicing

Some recipes call for chiles to be cut into lengthwise strips or '*rajas*'. In this case, clean chiles by slicing downward to create strips about 1/8" to 1/4" (.3-.6 mm) width (*half a small finger width*). Deveining and cleaning is easy when the recipe calls for strips. Just cut a chile open lengthwise and scrape out all seeds and veins before slicing into strips. Rinse the whole chile and slice *after* it dries on a paper towel. *Rajas* are marvelous toppers for any cheese, egg, or salad recipe.

Stuffing

When chiles are used for stuffing more care is required during roasting and peeling. First of all, look for the best quality chiles in the market (fresh, nice shape, and firm flesh). Be extra gentle when roasting and cleaning so as not to tear into the flesh. And, leave the stem in place— it looks great on the plate. Buy a few extra and prepare more than a recipe suggests.

Storing roasted chiles

Roasted and prepared chiles can be stored in their juice in the refrigerator for a few days. Put them in a small, covered bowl and cover with clear kitchen wrap or a tight lid. Do not cover the chiles until they are thoroughly cooled. Otherwise, they continue to cook and become soggy.

For detailed information on other special storing techniques like freezing, canning and pickling, check out pages 44 or 147.

All roasted chiles are put aside to 'sweat' after roasting.

They can be covered with towels, put in a plastic bag, or in a brown paper bag.

This roasted Anaheim has just been removed from a brown paper bag, and the outer membrane has slightly separated from the underlying juicy flesh.

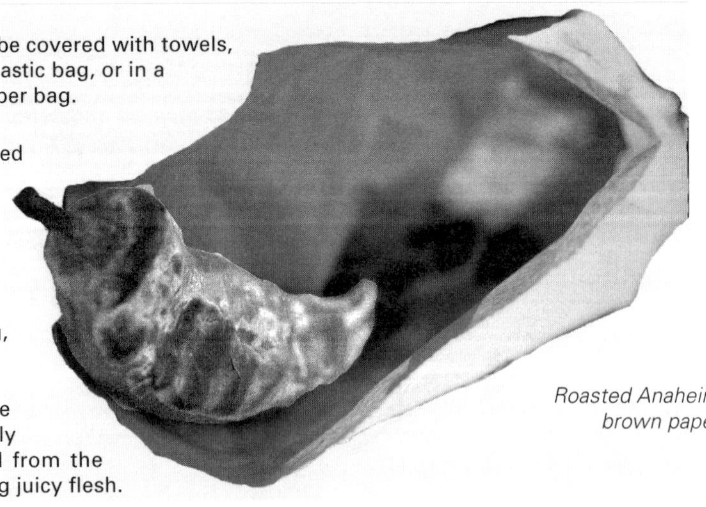

Roasted Anaheim chile in a brown paper bag

It will be easy to peel the outer layer from this chile.

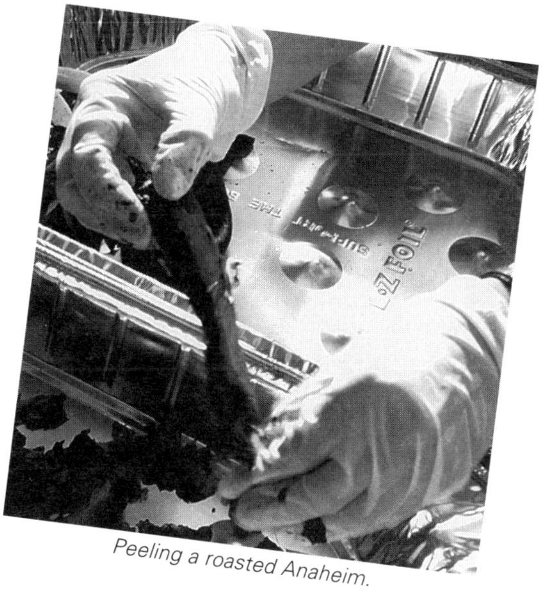

Peeling a roasted Anaheim.

It is easy to peel chiles which have been roasted and allowed to sweat. Hold the chile at the stem and slide your hand down toward the tip. The outer membrane should peel away.

Rinse the peeled chile in cool water to remove any remaining traces of the outer layer.

Roasting and Peeling Tips

- Cook chiles by broiling in normal ovens, toaster ovens, in frying pans, over gas flame, or on the barbecue.
- Cook chiles until skin blisters and separates from flesh.
- Turn frequently so that all sides are roasted and colour change is uniform.
- Do not overcook— chiles will become soft and difficult to manage.
- After all sides blister, place in a thick-plastic or a brown-paper bag. Close, and let sit for 15-20 minutes.
- When cool, remove and skin. Skin will rub off easily. For stubborn areas scrape lightly with a sharp paring knife.
- Stuffed chiles are often cooked after stuffing, so the trick is to roast these chiles just enough to burn off the skin. After roasting, place chile in ice water. This stops the cooking process and makes chile easier to handle for stuffing.
- Wear latex gloves if you are sensitive to capsaicin.

Commercial size roaster from back and front side.

These special roasters are capable of roasting large sacks of fresh Anaheim and New Mexico chiles. A flame spreader at the rear allows an intense flame to roast the chiles as they are rotated over the flame. Some of the outer skin burns off and is caught by a special flashing placed under the front side.

Snappies for Salsa

We call these three fresh chiles, the jalapeño, the serrano and the habanero the snappies. Why? Because all three are small, hot, and usually chopped up for salsa. And salsas are a snap to make, as you'll soon find out. In recent years salsas have become very popular. In fact, they've replaced ketchup as the condiment or 'relish' of choice. No wonder! Salsas are healthy, flavourful and free of fat.

A calavera is a skeleton, and the Jose Guadalupe Posada used them for political commentary 100 years ago. These two distinguished ladies are discussing the merits of a snappy serrano and a extra hot habanero. Serranos and jalapeños are Aztec chiles and the habaneros are Mayan.

The Snappies

Three fresh chiles— the *jalapeño*, the *serrano*, and the *habanero*— are now commonly available in most supermarkets. We've included some pictures to help you identify and recognize them.

The *jalapeño* and *serrano* are the most widely used fresh hot chiles. Although some cookbooks describe these two chile peppers as interchangeable— there are differences in both *appearance* and in *taste*. The *jalapeño* is larger, plumper and a deeper green than the serrano. The *serrano* is smaller, has a thinner skin, is less fleshy and is often not as shiny as the jalapeño. Sometimes the jalapeño is available in a beautiful red colour and, in this state it is a wonderful chile for preserving. But most often, both the jalapeño and serrano are sold in their green skins. These two chiles also differ in taste! The *jalapeño* has a more complex flavour while the *serrano* is usually hotter and more piquant. The jalapeño is like a fine white Bordeaux wine and the serrano more like a Riesling.

Lucky for everyone, the *habanero's* appearance is very distinctive. Habaneros have surface indentations and grooves and come in a wide range of colours— including light to deep green, bright red, and brilliant yellow. But every habanero is very, very hot! It's about 100 times hotter than the jalapeño. Never use this little gem without knowing exactly what you're dealing with. If you want a salsa that's *muy picante*, then this is the one— but use it *sparingly*. Its exotic fruity flavour will be lost if your mouth is on fire. Although the habanero is often referred to as a 'scotch bonnet', these are actually two different albeit closely related chiles.

Serrano chile pepper, larger jalapeño chile pepper, and habanero chile pepper.

If a habanero were a white wine it would definitely be a Chardonnay!

These three chiles, the *jalapeño, serrano* and *habanero* are the basic *salsa chiles*. Whether fresh or roasted, they are chopped, blended or puréed with other ingredients to make a whole range of tasty salsas, which are used as dips, dressings or condiments.

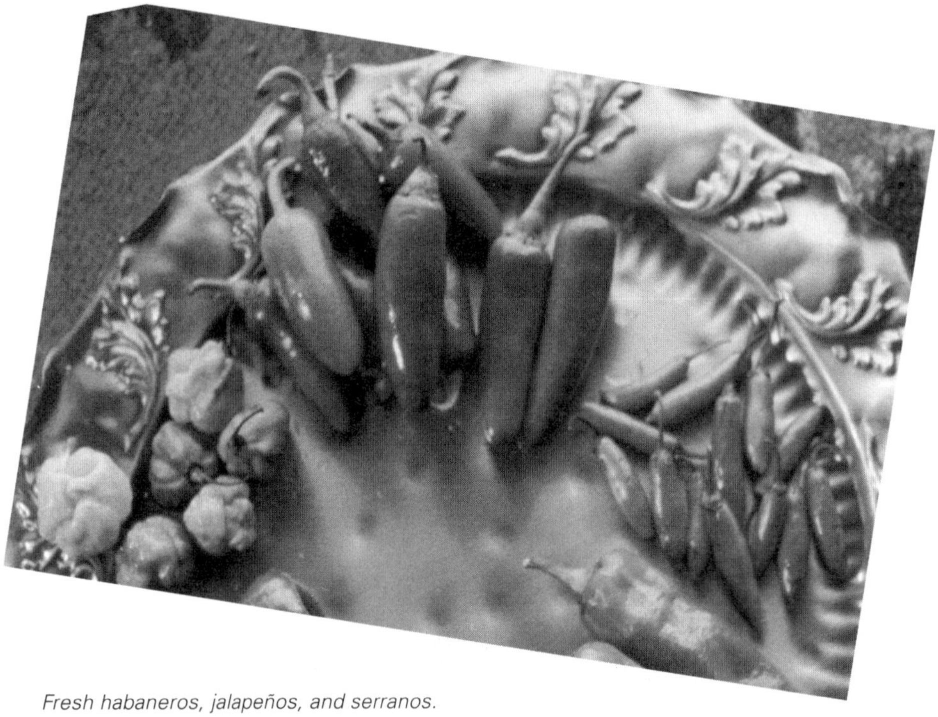

Fresh habaneros, jalapeños, and serranos.

The people of the Yucatan commonly use the habanero as an essence and flavouring as much as they use it as a whole hot chile. Habaneros are halved and placed in a liquid with other ingredients, and its capsaicin diffuses into everything else. Onions, carrots, and radishes take on the extra heat provided by the chile. Often, rather than eat the habanero, they 'dab' it with tortillas or bread and soak up a little bit of the juice. This technique has the intriguing name of making 'chuk'. Many have suggested that this technique is the best way to acclimatize one's tastebuds to the powerful kick of the habanero. Eventually, you might be able to eat one whole.

Green and red serranos.

Now let's look at each of the snappy chiles in detail, and then use each one in a few recipes.

The Jalapeño

If you've ever eaten *nachos* (*and who hasn't?*) you've already encountered the jalapeño in its pickled form. It *is* the most widely available chile in Canada and the US, and it's now sold fresh almost year round. If by some chance they aren't available fresh, they are *always* available in the pickled version in jars or cans. Jalapeños are about 2-3 inches (5-8 cm) long and are relatively fat and "fleshy". They're a deep shiny green, but shiny *red* ones are occasionally available.

Jalapeños are named after Jalapa (*Xalapa*)— a wonderful and interesting mountain city in the Mexican State of Vera Cruz. The citizens of this cultured city still proudly call themselves *Jalapeños*, and their soccer stadium is *Estadio Jalapeño*. In other parts of Vera Cruz jalapeños are called *gordos* (fat ones) and in Mexico City giant ones are *cuaresmeños*. There's also a very large version of the jalapeño from Southern Vera Cruz, Tabasco and Campeche known as the *huachinango*— perhaps because it is used to spice up *huachinango* (red snapper) dishes. For chile experts, there are as many variations in jalapeños as wine lovers find in fermented grapes.

North of the Mexican border jalapeños are commonly used in salsas or as a pickled condiment alongside a main dish. But in Mexico, they use the serrano for fresh salsas and about 60% of their fresh jalapeño crop is *processed*— that is, pickled, canned or used in bottled salsas. Another 20% are *smoked* to produce exotic chipotles (see page 133). Because they have fleshy bodies, jalapeños can mould before they fully dry in the open air— hence preservation by smoking. Interestingly, this smoking technique has changed little from that originally used by the first peoples of Mexico. (To read more about the chipotle and smoking techniques we *enthusiastically* refer you to Jacqueline Higuera McMahan's Chipotle Chile Cook Book.)

Most of us consider the jalapeño a very spicy chile. But when situated within the total range of chiles it actually *rates about a medium*. However, jalapeños vary individually in degree of heat, and Texas growers have even given birth to a "non-spicy" version. Furthermore, *stress* (e.g. drought or too much moisture) during cultivation adds more heat to chiles, and they are affected by dramatic shifts in climactic conditions during the growing season.

Jalapeños are also grown near Laredo, Texas where they celebrate the harvest with an annual jalapeño festival.

Texas A&M university has developed several new hybrids. One mild version looks like a jalapeño but has no 'bite'. The biotech mild version is actually a mixture of serrano and string chile— and has unfortunately contributed to more confusion about jalapeños.

So, *you'd best make note*! There is a wide range of heat levels for jalapeños and the only way to determine the exact heat level is to *sample* a chile. Manufacturers of canned and pickled versions try to indicate the *general level* of heat by printing a thermometer on the side of the bottle or tin. Obviously with fresh you take what you get!

Jalapeños are used *fresh* in salsas, but their fleshy bodies acquire wonderful flavours when roasted or pickled (*en escabeche*). They are perfect as a condiment for nachos, salads, beans and many other side dishes. They've also become popular as deep-fried appetizers— usually stuffed with beans or cheese. We devoured the most wonderful stuffed jalapeños in the beautiful city of Puebla, Mexico where giant 3 inch long versions are stuffed with melted Oaxaca cheese.

Diana Kennedy says that in her many years of cooking she has learned "with chiles you can never be quite sure what you've got".

Chiles reflect the temperature, climate and soil in which they're grown. And easy cross-pollination creates many varieties with unpredictable flavour and heat level.

Any extraordinary change during the growing season creates a trauma, which will make that particular crop even hotter!

Close-up view of jalapeños beside habaneros.

You might find a bright, red chile that looks very much like the jalapeño. It's probably a ***fresno*** and is a tad hotter then the jalapeño.

Actually, if you look carefully you can see that its shape is a little different; it is broader at the stem than at the tip. The fresno can add a touch of colour to your favorite salsa– but it also is very likely to add more heat.

Another common chile is the ***yellow hot wax chile.*** It's used in almost the same way as the jalapeño but is a little sweeter and doesn't have the eye-catching brightness of the fresno.

American agribusiness is continually searching for new varieties, and new hybrids appear on grocery shelves. Few are welcomed by traditional users.

Fresh Jalapeños can be preserved by smoking. This process creates the delicious chipotle chile. We'll tell you more about this when we discuss dried chiles.

Take it easy at first

A smart way to start using fresh jalapeños (and for that matter, any unfamiliar hot chile) is to add just a few at the start. Begin with one. Add one at a time, for additional heat and flavour.

Fresh Ingredients for snappy salsa recipes

One important ingredient in many of these recipes is cilantro, and unfortunately it is still relatively underappreciated in Canada and the USA. Mexicans have been using cilantro (culantro) for so long that they are convinced that it is one of the many ingredients that Mexico gave to the world. But, the Spanish introduced cilantro into Mexico and it was such a perfect complement that it was quickly adopted. Cilantro is widely available in supermarkets, although it is sometimes labeled as Chinese parsley or fresh coriander. Do not confuse it with parsley! It has a flatter leaf and a very different taste. By the way, you can keep it fresh in your refrigerator for several days by placing the stems in a glass of water and covering the leafy part of the cilantro with a plastic produce bag.

Now for some jalapeño recipes!

Well, let's move on to recipes using the jalapeño chile pepper.

Even though the recipes in this book use commonly available ingredients, you may see a few items that you don't recognize. To help you out with anything that looks unfamiliar we've provided a glossary on some pages, and you can check more detailed information about complements starting on page 151.

Snappy Recipes with Jalapeños

Here are two classic, and yet simple salsas. This first one is found throughout the Southwestern US and is known by many names including *Salsa Mexicana, Salsa Fresca,* or *Salsa Cruda.*

SALSA MEXICANA

It can be served simply as a dip with chips, nachos, crackers or pita. Or, it can add extra flavour to tacos, enchiladas and other Mexican dishes. Salsa Mexicana is also delicious on beans, or as a straight substitute for ketchup— on eggs, hamburgers, french fries and almost anything else. Roasting all of the ingredients gives this salsa a wonderful smoky quality. For a fresher, crunchier texture roast only the jalapeños. Varying the size of the chopped ingredients produces different effects. Most of the time, the individual pieces are relatively chunky. El Shrimp Bucket restaurant in Mazatlan makes this salsa fresh at your table while you are waiting for your entrée.

1 or 2 fresh jalapeños—roasted, peeled, stemmed and seeded

1/2 medium onion, sliced and roasted

2 cloves garlic, roasted

4 roasted tomatoes *(preferably roma or plum)*

1/4 cup cilantro

juice of 1 lime

salt to taste *(a pinch)*

Roast the jalapeños, onion, garlic and tomatoes until softened and charred. Let the ingredients cool a bit after roasting. Then place them in a blender or food processor along with all of the remaining ingredients. Chop or blend until you have a very chunky mixture. To produce a salsa with less liquid, chop the ingredients by hand. This makes about 2 cups.

Remember: this salsa is meant to be chunky, so go easy with the processor.

Roasting ingredients on a cast-iron comal

Depending on your preferences, chop the ingredients into small or large pieces. The Salsa Mexicana at the right was made by chopping the ingredients into large pieces.

Once you get the hang of this simple salsa, experiment with some variations or substitutions.

- Substitute one small can of whole Italian plum tomatoes for fresh tomatoes.
- Substitute green or red onion.
- Add small amounts of seasonings such as cumin or oregano. These seasonings can also be roasted lightly in a pan before you add them.
- Add green or red pepper for a sweeter taste. This is not authentic, but suits some palates.
- Use the fresno chile for more colour and a hotter bite.
- Use pickled jalapeños.
- Try chopping the ingredients into different sizes to produce a different texture.

Happy Note

Salsas are the answer to a dieter's prayer. They add tons of flavour with very little fat. Plus they are nutritious- filled with vitamins A,C, niacin, riboflavin and sodium. Salsas are perfect on salad- they add flavour without the fat!

SALSA VERDE *(Green Sauce)*

This classic is a salsa verde (green sauce) using tomatillos. It has a wonderful fresh taste and can be served as a relish or a topping for almost anything. You've seen tomatillos—those odd husked green things— in the produce section of your supermarket. Tomatillos are a staple of Mexican and southwestern salsas. When combined with chiles they add a fresh full flavour to the mix. For complete information on tomatillos please see page 151.

Tomatillos are almost always cooked before use. It's really easy to do! Just remove the papery husks and wash them until no longer sticky. Place them in a saucepan and barely cover them with water. Boil them for about 15 minutes until they become soft and yellow. Or you can also roast them in a skillet or broil them. Just make sure they are soft and squishy. That's it— they're ready to use. Some supermarkets carry canned tomatillos, which can be substituted for fresh in an emergency.

2 jalapeños, peeled, roasted, seeded and chopped

6–8 large fresh tomatillos, boiled or roasted

1/2 cup cilantro leaves, chopped

1 medium onion, roasted and cut into large pieces

2 or 3 garlic cloves, roasted

juice of one lime

1/2 tsp. crushed cumin seed *(optional)*

salt to taste

Combine everything in a food processor and chop to desired consistency. This salsa can be made extra chunky or chopped to a finer constituency. This recipe makes about 2 cups.

The cumin seed is a wonderful little addition, especially if the seeds are lightly roasted in a dry frying pan.

Limes in Mexico are very different than those we get in Canada and the USA. In Mexico, limes are sweet (like *Key Limes*). We're most likely to get *Persian Limes* which are more like lemons— that is sour. Add a dollop of honey to Persian lime juice before using. See page 155.

Salsa Verde *This will soon become one of your favourite salsas. Use a food processor and the 'pulse' setting. Keep the pulse bursts very short and the salsa will be chunky. Add a little bit of water if you would like a thinner salsa.*

Tomatillos: remove the papery husk and wash in cool water. They can be boiled in water— but are delicious roasted.

Homemade Barbecue Salsa Mixtures

These two salsas use the jalapeño and are perfect for barbecue fanatics. The first one adds a jalapeño twist to create a special barbecue sauce and is based on one described in the Whole Chile Book by Dave DeWitt and Nancy Gerlach. We describe this book on page 172.

A CHILE GRILL

This specific salsa is a tasty addition to barbecued chicken, or salmon. You can mix it with ground pork or beef for making your own special Sloppy Joe's.

6– 8 tomatoes, roasted, chopped and peeled *(optional)*

4 jalapeños–roasted, seeded and chopped

1 bell pepper, chopped

1 onion, chopped

1 cup brown sugar or honey

1 1/2 cups cider vinegar

3 tsp. ground cinnamon

2 tsp. of a fine dry mustard

dash of salt to taste

It is best to use a toaster oven for this recipe. Use the roasting pan that fits in your oven and set the temperature to about 375 degrees. Roast the tomatoes under the broiler for 10-15 minutes. Drain off the excess liquid from the tomatoes, and add the remaining fresh ingredients (jalapeños, bell pepper, and onion) to the pan with the tomatoes. Continue to roast the vegetable mixture for about one hour.

When everything is cooked, let the ingredients cool slightly and pour everything into a blender or food processor. Add the remaining dry ingredients and process until puréed. This makes about 3 cups of a wonderful barbecue type sauce.

Note: the idea is to make a smooth mixture with few chunks.

HELL'S A POPPIN' JALAPEÑO SALSA

This second barbecue salsa will give you real heat and a strong jalapeño flavour. It's simple to make and perfect with steaks. Just before you put the steaks on the grill, roast the chiles, onion, garlic and cumin, put them in the blender and process.

8–10 jalapeños, roasted, peeled, stemmed and chopped

1 onion, roasted and chopped

2 cloves garlic, roasted and minced

1 tbs. cumin

1 tbs. olive oil

1/4 cup water

Combine everything in a non-metallic dish and chop by hand. You can also use a food processor or blender. Makes about 1 cup.

Note: unlike most others, this salsa *contains* oil.

Hot and Cool Together!

JALAPEÑO CREAM SAUCE

Do you remember the first time you tried sweet and sour Chinese dishes? In Mexico, it is also common to mix contrasting tastes while cooking, but they mix "picante" and "cool" together with amazing results. If you love the flavour of jalapeños, but want to avoid the bite, try one of these next salsas. The use of cream or fruit does moderate the heat level. Or, to further reduce the heat you can soak the chiles in salt water, rinse them, and then do a second soak in cream before processing. This salsa is used as a dip, or as an incredible topping for baked potatoes and other vegetables. Try it with chicken wings or stuffed jalapeños.

2 fresh jalapeños, roasted, peeled, seeded and chopped

2 cloves garlic, roasted and minced

1 cup sour cream, yogurt or a combination of the two.

2 sprigs of fresh cilantro, finely chopped

1 tsp. oil

squirt of lime

ground pepper to taste

Combine all ingredients and refrigerate for 1 or 2 hours before serving. This will keep in the refrigerator for several days covered tightly.

Mexicans use a **crema fresca**. This is a rich and heavy cream that is slightly thinned. A mixture of 1/2 cup buttermilk and 1/2 cup of sour cream is a good substitute. But, to reduce fat content where crema or sour cream is called for, we substitute low fat yogurt (e.g. Yoplait). California's Mexican cuisine maintained the preference for heavy creams and rich sour cream.

MANGO JALAPEÑO SALSA

Mango, jalapeño and cilantro create an absolute taste sensation when combined. Serve this exotic mixture with chicken, pork or fish. It's also great with such Asian appetizers as gyozas, crispy spring rolls, or deep fried won tons. The mango is another non-native food that Mexicans have made their own.

2- 3 fresh jalapeños, roasted, peeled, seeded and chopped

2 ripe mangos, peeled and chopped (*or a whole pineapple or mixture of both*)

1 white or red onion, finely chopped

1/2 cup cilantro leaves, chopped

1-2 cloves of garlic, chopped

juice of one lime

1/2 red bell pepper, finely chopped (*optional*)

Combine all ingredients and refrigerate for 1 or 2 hours before serving. The mango has a big flat pit. Peel off the outer skin, and make a series of deep cross-cuts in the mango every 1/4"; then, slide the knife along the pit surface to cut off the fruit pieces from the pit. With practice, you'll create perfectly diced pieces of mango for this salsa. Makes 3-4 cups. Keeps 1-2 days in the refrigerator.

Variations

- **Add a few chopped walnuts for extra texture.**
- **Add a dash of tequila for an extra special flavour.**
- **Substitute serranos for the jalapeños.**

Snappy Starters!

Although jalapeños are primarily used in salsas, they spice up other dishes as well. Try the next two delicious appetizers! One is a classic guacamole in which the jalapeño provides a sharp counterpoint to the marvelous, rich flavour of the avocado. No fattening mayo or sour cream is needed. The second recipe uses cream cheese, which you can use as described or thin the cheese with yogurt without losing much flavour. Both of these recipes are fabulous and are great with chips, crackers and veggies.

GUACAMOLE

1 jalapeño chile, roasted and chopped with seeds

2 ripe avocados, peeled and chopped

1 plum tomato, chopped

1 tbs. minced fresh onion

2 garlic cloves, minced

4 sprigs of fresh cilantro, chopped

dash of oregano and cumin

squirt of lime

salt to taste (*optional*)

Cut the avocado into small chunks: to do this, remove the skin and make a series of deep cuts across and down the entire avocado, and then slice off all of the little cubes. Mix in the chile, tomato, onion, cilantro and garlic. We like it chunky and try to 'mix' it, but some people like to mash it and others make a purée. Add the oregano and lime. To keep the avocado from turning brown, leave the pit buried in the mixture until you are ready to serve the dip. Makes one cup.

Read more about the avocado on page 155.

Ingredients in a bowl ready for mashing or mixing to taste

Avocado: More varieties of avocados are available in Mexico than in other parts of North America. They're often referred to as *manteca de los pobres* (the poor people's butter)— but in this case, the poor are better off because avocados don't have the unhealthy cholesterol (LDL) of the dairy product. According to hip healthster Dr. Andrew Weill, avocados provide good cholesterol (HDL).

JALAPEÑO CREAM CHEESE

Whip cream cheese. (Reduce the cream cheese to 2 oz and add about half a small yogurt cup if you are watching fat content.) Add the jalapeño and onion. Makes one cup.

1 jalapeño, roasted, peeled, seeded and finely chopped

4 oz. cream cheese

1/4 cup red onion, finely chopped

SHRIMP SUPREME

Here's a marvelous stuffing for fresh corn tortillas. It's taken from Patricia Quintana's The Taste of Mexico and is used to make tacos de Escuinapa— a specialty of Escuinapa, Sinaloa where the native shrimp are magnificent. Notice that the cilantro is ***removed*** *from the mixture before serving.*

Heat the oil in a frying pan and brown the garlic. Brown the onion and then add the jalapeños, tomatoes, and the cilantro bunch, shrimp and a dash of salt. Cook until the mixture thickens. Remove the cilantro, and serve on fresh tortillas.

3/4 cup vegetable oil

4 garlic coves, whole

1 1/2 whole white onions, chopped

4 jalapeños, roasted, peeled, deseeded and chopped

5 tomatoes, chopped

30 sprigs of cilantro, tied in a bunch with a string

1 3/4 lbs. shrimp, shelled, deveined and finely chopped

dash of salt

Cilantro: A leafy plant, sometimes called ***chinese parsley*** or ***fresh coriander***. It was introduced into Mexico, but no one is certain how it arrived. Although It was popular in Spain (because of the Moorish influence), some have suggested that cilantro was actually introduced to Mexico via the Spanish colonalization of the Philippines.

Keep cilantro fresh by trimming the roots, and place it in a glass of water in your refrigerator. Cover lightly with a plastic bag. Generally, we prefer the leaves and not the stems. See page 154.

TOPOPO

Well, we just can't leave the good old jalapeño without including one of our favorite recipes. The topopo is a salad in a cone shape like a volcano— named after Mexico's famous Popocatépetl. This salad, built on top of a fried tortilla, is topped with pickled jalapeño strips. The topopo is a favorite at Mexican restaurants (like La Fuente or El Minuto) in Tucson, Arizona.

1 corn tortilla deep-fried in a pan until golden and crisp.

3 tbs. of refried beans

2 cups of head lettuce, shredded

1 can of mixed vegetables

1 breast of chicken, in strips

1/2 avocado, cut in strips

pickled jalapeño strips

1 slice tomato (beefsteak)

1 tbs. cottage cheese

***dressing* (Salsa Mexican, Italian)**

Spread the refried beans on corn tortilla. Mix the shredded lettuce with one can of mixed vegetables (peas, carrots, and potatoes) and pile all of this on top of beans and tortilla. This dish is supposed to resemble a mountain, so you just keep piling up the goodies. Alternate strips of chicken, avocado and the jalapeño on sides of lettuce. Finally, top with slice of tomato and cottage cheese.

For a salad dressing, use either light Italian or the *Salsa Mexicana* described on page 33.

Did you know that corn tortillas have absolutely no oil added to them? Flour tortillas, while delicious, contain oil. In fact, the most authentic ones are made with lard.

San Xavier Mission near Tucson Arizona.
The Topopo is served in many restaurants in this area

Popocatépetl: A volcano, 60 km from Mexico City, which recently resumed activity. Local people believe that *Popo* is alive and has the name *Don Goyo*. *Popocatépetl* is the counterpart of Romeo (or Tristan). Popocatépetl's legend is a sad story about fated lovers. A war chief, *Popocatépetl* came back from battle to find his beloved *Ixtaccihuatl* (a neighbouring dormant volcano) lying in death and chose to lay beside her forever.

There are many other ways to use jalapeños

- Jalapeños are used mostly in salsas. But they're also delicious stuffed with cheese and served as an appetizer. For information on stuffing jalapeños please refer the Stuffers chapter– pages 65.
- Chopped up in refried beans.
- Stuffed with cheese, beans or peanut butter and deep fried.
- In spreads and dips.
- In marinades.
- Pickled as a condiment on just about anything.
- Refer to our recommended cookbooks at the end of this book (page 169). These contain many jalapeño recipes .

Canning Jalapeños

If you are willing to go beyond the simple techniques for preserving chiles described on page 146, you might consider canning (also known as pickling). First, it is necessary to remind everyone about basic preparation techniques for safe canning.

Here are two relatively uncomplicated canning recipes if you have the equipment and are confident in your ability to can safely .

JALAPEÑOS EN ESCABECHE

En escabeche simply means 'pickled chiles'. Jalapeños en escabeche are a particular favorite, and in fact it is these pickled chiles which are most often used on the ubiquitous nachos.

enough jalapeños to fill pint size canning jars

sliced carrots

chunks of onions

1/2 tsp. salt per pint

1 clove garlic minced per pint jar

5% white vinegar and water in equal amounts

fine olive oil

Wash the jalapeños and remove the stems. Prick or slash the jalapeños in several places. Add to the jars, and put in some of the sliced carrots, chunks of onions and minced garlic. Mix enough liquid (50-50) to completely cover the ingredients and come to 3/4" below the rim of the jar. Add a thin layer of olive oil to the top (about 1/8"). Wipe the rim clean, and put on a sterilized ring and lid. Place in 170°F (77°C) water, making sure that the tops of the jars are covered. Maintain at this temperature for 15 minutes. Carefully remove the jar, and wipe the tops. Let cool, and test lids to see if they are tightly sealed. The lids are slightly concave when properly sealed.

Store in a cool place at no more than 75°F (24°C).

CANNED GREEN SALSA

This is a wonderful canned version of the simple green salsa that we told you about at the beginning of this chapter. Because vinegar is added, it tastes a little different. However, these canned versions are infinitely better than commercial ones sold in supermarkets. During the short and cold days of winter this salsa lifts the spirits and warms the soul.

5 lb. (2 kg) of tomatillos

1 lb. (250 gr.) onions, chopped

6 cloves of garlic, minced

2 lb. (800 gr.) fresh jalapeño, finely chopped

2 tsp. salt

3/4 cup (800 ml) 5% white vinegar

1/2 cup (100 g) finely chopped cilantro

Pick the tomatillos carefully (see pages 35 & 151). Avoid those with bruises. De-husk them and wash them carefully. Cover with cold water in a heavy pot, and heat until the water boils. Cook about 15 minutes, or until the tomatillos have turned translucent. Discard the water, and place the tomatillos in a blender/processor. Process until tomatillos are slightly chunky. Put all remaining ingredients except for the cilantro in the cooking pot and heat for 5 minutes. Add the chopped cilantro and stir. Put the cooked mixture in small canning jars, leaving 1/2 inch (1.2 cm) of space from the rim. Carefully wipe the top of each jar. Put on the sterilized rings and lids. Put jars in the kettle, and make sure that the water is 170ºF and that it completely covers the jars. Leave in this bath at this temperature for 15 minutes. Carefully remove the jars, and wipe. Let cool and confirm that the lid is sealed. The lids are concave after cooling.

This makes about 7 pints, or about 4 litres of salsa. If you can't fit it all in the jars, you can use the leftover cooked salsa over the next few days.

Variations

- Add a little toasted and crushed cumin seed to the mixture after cooking. You can also add 1/2 teaspoon of golden *tequila* or *mescal* for an extra special salsa.
- The tomatillos can be roasted before adding the vinegar.

Safe Canning Procedures

• Be sure to properly sterilize canning jars and lids.

• Follow instructions included with canning jars and lids.

• Never use chipped or cracked jars.

• Follow recipes exactly— fill the jars as described in the recipes.

• Remove all air bubbles before putting lids on the jars.

• Clean the rim carefully before putting tops on jars.

• Use canning kettles or deep pots with a rack on bottom.

• The kettle must be deep enough to cover tops of the jars.

• Heat the water to 170°F (77°C) before inserting jars.

• Place the filled jars in hot water and process at that temperature for the time listed in the recipe.

• Make sure that jar tops are perfectly sealed after removing from the water.

• Store in a cool, dry and preferably dark place. The temperature should not get above 75°F (24°C).

• An excellent overview of canning is found in the California Culinary Academy Book, Mexican Cooking at the Academy.

Other chiles can also be canned with great success.

• Red jalapeños make beautiful jars of chiles.

• Serranos are commonly pickled.

The Serrano

Well, now that you know how to use the snappy jalapeño, the snappy serrano will be— well, a *snap*. Serrano literally means "*from the mountains*" and that's where this little chile grows. Although we're more familiar with the jalapeño, in Mexico the serrano is *the* chile of choice for salsas. And now it's much more readily available in big supermarkets.

How does the serrano differ from the jalapeño?

It's a bit hotter, smaller— about 1-1/2 inches long (4 cm)— and less fleshy. The serrano is a medium-green colour; it's cylindrical in shape and more pointed at one end. Like the jalapeño, serranos ripen to a bright red. But because it's less fleshy, the serrano is air dried like other fresh chiles. It is possible to find a dried serrano, but not in regular supermarkets. A substitute for the dried version of a serrano is a similar chile called the "*chile de arbol*". But, we're getting ahead of ourselves and we'll wait to tell you more about that in the *dried* chiles section.

The serrano has a fresh, sharp taste— and because it's small, is rarely deseeded or deveined. The seeds add a piquant flavour to the dishes that use this chile. It's most commonly used as a *fresh ingredient* in table salsas, where it packs a real wallop and adds a considerable amount of heat to a mixture.

If you want to use them in *cooked sauces*, toast them until the skin blisters and becomes soft. Then, you can store them in the refrigerator in a covered bowl until needed. Don't forget there's no need to peel these little guys— they're too small and the skin is very thin.

Serranos are pickled and canned, but these aren't readily available in Canada and the USA. Some supermarkets do sell *pickling chiles* which bear a resemblance— but these are longer and thinner with more sharply pointed tips. Be forewarned these are not good substitutes for serranos and they don't have the sharp flavour unique to the Mexican beauty.

When serranos are used, it is very common to slice them into thin 'rings'. This is done by cutting them across the chile instead of lengthwise.

Recipes with Serranos

PICO DE GALLO

Let's start with a definitive serrano salsa that's on virtually every table in Mexico City. It's called Pico de Gallo, which literally means the rooster's beak— perhaps a reference to the shape, size and appearance of serranos. Here's our version of this popular salsa. As always, the ingredients can be roasted or grilled for that extra flavour.

4 fresh serrano chiles, roasted and chopped

6 medium plum tomatoes, chopped *(option: peeled)*

1/2 cup white or red onion, finely chopped

1/3 cup cilantro, chopped

dash of lime juice

pinch of salt to taste

Combine all the ingredients.

This salsa can be served as a condiment with almost anything. In Mexico, you'll see it served on quesadillas, in soups, on eggs and anything else. Keep in mind this is a fresh salsa so we suggest you make it in small batches. It will only last a few days in the fridge.

The recipe makes about 1 cup.

Pico de Gallo Variations

- **All ingredients can be roasted, to create a big taste difference.**
- **Add 1 tsp. of olive oil for a slightly different flavour.**
- **Leave out the tomatoes for a greener, less hearty version.**
- **Add white onion to the blender first and process this first. Then add the other ingredients and pulse in short bursts. This two step blending produces a whiter and creamier salsa.**

SALSA VERDE WITH TOMATILLOS

Remember the salsa verde recipe with jalapeños on page 35? That same recipe can be made with serranos. This next salsa verde can also be used with either jalapeños or serranos. The difference is that it's cooked after it is mixed and blended. This recipe is based on one in "Bienvenidos to Our Kitchen" by Luis and Marilyn Peinado—another of our recommended cookbooks. It's easy to make and can be used in many ways. See our suggestions in the box which follows.

15 tomatillos

4-6 serrano chiles

1/2 onion

1/2 tsp. oregano leaves

2 tsp. fresh chopped garlic

2 sprigs of fresh cilantro

salt to taste

also: 3 tbs. canola oil *for heating*

Remove the husks from tomatillos (see page 152). Rinse under cool running water. Place a 5-quart pot 1/2 full of water on stove and bring to boil. Add the rinsed tomatillos to pot of boiling water, reduce the heat to medium, and let tomatillos simmer for 5-10 minutes, or until they are just tender. Remove tomatillos from hot water with slotted spoon.

In blender grind tomatillos, chiles, onion, garlic and oregano with 1/4-cup water, being careful not to overblend. Use the pulse setting in short bursts. Add the rinsed cilantro leaves (do not use stems) and turn blender on and off three times. Heat oil in heavy frying pan, add tomatillo sauce, and simmer for 5-8 minutes. Adjust salt.

Serves 4- 6.

The ingredients for salsa verde on a roasting pan. The tomatillos in this version can be roasted instead of cooked in water

Green Salsa Variations

• The ingredients can be roasted for that extra bit of flavour.

• Just remove husks from tomatillos, rinse and place along with chiles and onion under broiler or on hot griddle. Roast until they brown. Place in blender and continue as above.

• Use this salsa verde to whip up a simple main dish called enchiladas verdes.

*Take a few corn tortillas, dip them in oil, and fill them with cooked chicken.

*Wrap and place in casserole dish. Then top the enchiladas with the salsa verde, and cover everything with a touch of heavy cream or a yogurt/cream combination (optional).

* Heat in the oven at 375° F for about 15 minutes or until heated through.

*Serve with condiments– onions, cilantro, and oregano.

•For a quick' n easy snack, top a small round piece of soft, white cheese with this salsa verde and heat it up in the oven. Serve with crackers. This salsa can also be used for chilaquiles– see the recipe on page 51.

Tortillas: We'll say a bit more about tortillas later (page 156). It is difficult to find authentic corn or flour tortillas outside of Mexico. Supermarket tortillas are *thicker* and *less tasty* than an authentic version. Look for the thinnest flour tortilla available, and fry it in a little corn oil to soften it. As for corn tortillas—under no circumstance buy yellow tortilla shells. Look for corn tortillas at a Latin store , or make tortillas using masa seca. Contrary to American and Canadian impressions, a basic corn tortilla is very white.

CHILAQUILES VERDES

In Mexico, most everyone buys their tortillas fresh daily. Preservatives are not used and tortillas are not refrigerated. Those left at the end of the day are considered stale. They are often used the next morning for a wonderful Mexican version of hash called chilaquiles. There are many versions of this dish, —but one of the most popular uses salsa verde. Simply combine the stale tortillas with salsa verde and chicken (if you wish),— and voilá. Serve the chilaquiles topped with cheese.

oil for cooking

8 dry corn tortillas, broken into large pieces and fried in oil until golden brown

1 cup of fresh salsa verde

1 cup water

1 cup chicken consommé

crumbly white cheese

***or substitute:* half container of plain low-fat yogurt**

Make the salsa verde described in the previous recipe (Salsa Verde with Tomatillos page 49). Heat the oil in a pan and lightly fry the tortillas until golden but not too crisp. Set aside on a paper towel. Add a little more oil to coat the pan, heat and add the salsa mixture to it. Stir, and immediately add chicken consommé and water until you have produced a thick but runny liquid. Add the fried tortilla pieces into this mixture and stir. Pour everything into casserole dish and top with crumbly white cheese as a topping. The pieces of chicken may also be added for extra flavour at the same time as you add the broth to the frying pan. Some people spread fresh cream over the top— but we suggest you add a little fresh yogurt after the dish has been assembled.

ISLAND SALSA

Here's a fruity serrano mix— a taste and visual sensation!

2 serranos, roasted and minced

1 cup pineapple, chopped

2 cups mango, peeled and chopped

1 cup yellow or red bell pepper, chopped

2/3 cup kiwi fruit, peeled and chopped

1/2 red onion, finely chopped

1/4 cup fresh cilantro, chopped

1 tsp. lime juice

Collect all the ingredients in a mixing bowl. If desired, add salt and pepper to taste. Mango adds a wonderful tropical flavour to this salsa. This is a great complement for chicken and pork dishes. It is even better when chilled.

SERRANO PESTO

Serranos really liven up your favorite pasta. This version of a pesto sauce uses serranos and substitutes cilantro for the Italian parsley found in the continental version. The pesto has a rich and full-bodied flavour. This is a welcome innovation from outside Mexico.

4 serrano chiles, *(optional: roasted and seeded)*

3 bell peppers, roasted and seeded

3 cloves garlic, crushed

1/2 cup cilantro

2/3 cup piñon nuts *(pine nuts, or pignola from Italian sections of stores)*

1 cup fine olive oil

1 cup romano or high quality parmesan cheese (grated)

Mix all of the ingredients except the olive oil and cheese in your food processor or blender. Purée them until they are in small pieces, and then gradually add the olive oil by pouring into the 'spout' of your processor. Finally, gradually add the grated cheese to this mixture. Store this in the refrigerator after making it. Use with any pasta, but it goes particularly well with small pastas like rotini or fusili.

Snappy Serrano Snacks

The word ceviche comes from the verb *cebar*, meaning to saturate. Ceviche marinates in the refrigerator about one day before serving. Because of water impurities, it can be chancy trying the wonderful varieties of ceviche available at food stands in Mexico. But, do try them in restaurants where the water supplies are more carefully controlled.

One of the most popular '*antojitos*' (or snacks) in coastal regions of Mexico is *ceviche*. In South America, they believe that the 'aji' chile was made by God to be used in this dish. But in Mexico, there are many versions of this delicious seafood concoction using the serrano instead of the aji. In Mexico City, street vendors sell many versions of ceviche, and it is available in bulk in delicatessens. As you can imagine, there are many different recipes for *ceviche*.

CEVICHE

This ceviche from Acapulco, Guerrero is our favorite. It's similar to a version found in the magnificent, colourful, and tantalizing cookbook which is appropriately called- Mexico, the Beautiful. We often add a few slices of jalapeño to the serranos. And for a slightly heartier fish taste, throw in a can of drained shrimp, crab or tuna. Or use all three for a ceviche supreme. In Vera Cruz, they serve a wonderful version of this ceviche that includes melt-in-your mouth octopus.

2 lb. (1 kg) of fine quality red snapper fillets, cut into 1/2" cubes

2 cups (500 ml) fresh lime juice

1/3 cup (80ml) olive oil

3 cloves garlic

2 lb. (1 kg) ripe tomatoes (plum)

2 tbs. finely chopped pickled serranos or jalapeños (or fresh, roasted)

1 cup (250g) chopped onion

1/3 cup (15 g) chopped fresh cilantro

1/2 cup (125 ml) ketchup

1 tbs. dried oregano

1/2 cup (90g) chopped green olives

dash of salt and pepper

Place the fish in glass bowl, and cover it with lime. Marinate at room temperature for 2 1/2 hours. In warm weather, do not allow it to sit unrefrigerated for longer than 1 hour,— put it in the refrigerator for the final 1 1/2 hours of marination. Just before assembly, heat the oil in a fry pan; add the garlic and sauté for about 3 minutes. Discard the garlic pieces and let the oil cool slightly.

Chop the tomatoes and place them in a separate glass bowl. Add the onion, cilantro, ketchup, oregano, salt, pepper, the chiles and the olives. Combine with a spoon. Then, you should rinse the fish several times in cold water and let it drain on a paper towel. Add the fish to the tomato mixture and cover tightly with a clear wrap or aluminum foil. Let stand in refrigerator for one day before serving.

Serve with high quality crackers.

SHREDDED FISH

1/2 cup butter

1/2 cup olive oil

1 1/2 medium white onion, chopped

4 large ripe tomatoes, chopped

8 fresh serranos, chopped

1 1/2 lb or about 3 cups red snapper, perch or bass, steamed, shredded with liquid pressed out

1 tsp. oregano

juice of one lime cilantro

Here's another fish mixture, a tad richer than ceviche, but also perfect with tortillas, crackers, rolls or chips. You can also use shrimp, or crab in much the same way.

Heat oil and butter. Add onions, tomatoes, chiles and sautée. Add shredded fish. Add the oregano and lime. Season with salt and pepper, if desired. Cook until the liquid is absorbed. Serve on a platter, garnished with cilantro. Makes 3- 4 cups.

BLACK BEAN RELISH

1 serrano chile, seeded and chopped

1 can black beans (15 oz), rinsed and drained or 2 cups fresh cooked black beans.

1 medium tomato, finely chopped

1/2 cup chopped red bell pepper

1/4 cup chopped red onion

2 tbs. white wine vinegar

1 tbs. vegetable oil

There are many versions of black bean relish. Here's one we like. It's simple, yet tasty and can be prepared quickly to serve as an appetizer or condiment.

Combine all the ingredients and let them stand for a while before serving. Makes 2- 3 cups.

antojito: snacks, often made by street vendors in Mexico City and elsewhere. They can be tacos, quesadillas, tortas, and tamales. Some vendors specialize in only one type of tortilla dish.
tapas: are the snacks served with drinks, and this is the name preferred in bars and restaurants.
botanas: finger foods or snacks served with drinks.

The Habanero

If you like salsa to hurt— then the habanero is for you. To put things in perspective, it's— oh, about *100 times hotter* than a jalapeño. It's a favorite among chile heads at the Fiery Food Shows in Albuquerque, New Mexico. The habanero (sometimes referred to as a scotch bonnet) has a very distinctive flavour that can be described as *fruity* or *citrus*—like. It's shaped like a lantern or a tiny pumpkin and can be green, yellow orange or even purple depending on its degree of ripeness. Most habaneros are used fresh in salsas and are also found in chutneys.

Habanero literally means *of Havana* in reference to Havana, Cuba. It's thought to have originated somewhere in the Antilles and is still prevalent throughout the Caribbean and down towards Brazil. The trade winds and currents which run from Florida to the northern coast of South America correspond to the range of these superhot chiles. The jerk sauces of the Caribbean use habaneros for their kick.

These days, habaneros are grown extensively in Belize and in the Yucatan region of Southeastern Mexico. The Mexican dishes that use the habanero are based on an Antilles or a Mayan influence, whereas almost all of the other chiles in this book are linked to Aztec culinary traditions.

In the Yucatan, table condiments always include a habanero dish. But the locals often do not eat the actual chile. *Halved* chiles are placed in salsa dishes in order to imbue a picante quality *to the marinade* or *to other ingredients* such as sliced onions, carrots or radishes. The *Yucatecos* (people of the Yucatan) *'dab'* at habaneros with their tortilla or bread-rolls, and they name this delicate technique *'making chuk'*. Unsuspecting tourists rarely catch on, and often bite into the half-habanero. ***Ouch***! After the surprise, they usually order two additional bottles of hearty Yucateco beer.

Habaneros or scotch bonnets can be purchased at many supermarkets in Canada or the USA. If you have trouble finding them, try an Asian market.

Most recipes based on habaneros originate in the more tropical areas of Mexico, which are sometimes referred to as *Maya*land. In the next few pages we will provide a few Mayan recipes to sample.

A city in Belize called Melinda is home to a famous hot sauce operation owned and operated by Marie and Gerry Sharp. They cultivate their own chiles for use in their bottled salsa called– you guessed it– Melinda's. Their habanero sauce is in great demand because of its unique flavour. They also add carrots, which makes Melinda's a bit milder than other habanero sauces.

Their story appears to be a modern version of the McIlhenny story, where the American soldier took a chile from Mexico to Louisiana and contributed to the famous hot pepper sauce business.

There are at least 100 different chile types available in Mexico. All are varieties of *Capsicum annum* except for habaneros! Botanists assign them a unique category, *Capsicum chinense*.

Snappy Recipes with Habaneros

WORLD'S HOTTEST TABLE SALSA

Here is a salsa recipe from the Yucatan. Unless your taste buds have been highly sensitized, you will not be able to tell this from the extra hot version of Melinda's bottled sauce.

12 chopped habanero chiles, with stems removed

1/2 cup of chopped onion

2 cloves of garlic, minced

1 tbsp. canola oil

1/2 cup grated carrots

1/2 cup distilled vinegar

1/4 cup of lime juice

This is a really, *really*, *really* hot habanero salsa, of which there are many. Sautée the onion and garlic until golden and soft. Add the habaneros and the carrots to the mixture with a small amount of water. Bring to a boil, and reduce the heat until the carrots have softened. Place all of this in your processor and blend until it is smooth. Put the purée back into a pot, and then add the vinegar and lime juice. Heat for 5 minutes, and stand back from the escaping fumes.

Other recipes use this basic combination and add other ingredients. Some of them use pumpkin seeds (shelled and softened in the hot oil), others use juice from Seville oranges instead of the vinegar, some use only lime juice. The common ingredient of course is the habañero.

If you decide to be different, you can roast habaneros, but always be wary of the fumes. They will burn your face and eyes.

SIMPLY HABANERO

We've roasted habaneros but, as you can imagine, we try to be extra careful with these little bombshells. Here's a simple habanero table salsa to give you a 'feel' for the power of the habanero. It's a staple in the beautiful Yucatan colonial city of Merida.

1 habanero, roasted and chopped

cilantro

lime juice

dash of salt

Combine all ingredients. You can add it the top of any dish, but the natives simply *dip* a tortilla or bread roll into the liquid to add a bit of kick.

HABANERO TABLE SALSA

As mentioned earlier, combining hot chiles with fruit controls the heat. However, the habanero is in a class by itself and not much can be done to moderate its punch. Notwithstanding, it's citrus-like flavour is a perfect complement for pineapple, mango and other tropical fruits. Here's a very simple fruity table salsa. It uses the juice of bitter orange or Seville oranges (naranja agria) found in the Yucatan. Grapefruit juice with a touch of lime juice is a good substitute.

2 fresh habaneros roasted and chopped

juice of one bitter orange *or* 1/2 grapefruit spiced with lime

20– 30 sprigs cilantro, chopped

1 large red or white onion finely chopped

Mix all ingredients in a glass bowl and let stand for several hours before serving. This sauce is perfect with seafood, grilled meats and beans, tortillas, and eggs.

SALSA HABANERO Y COL

Arturo Lomeli wrote a splendid little book (in Spanish) called The Art of Cooking with Chile. He is a Mexican psychologist and provides several anecdotes about the culture of chiles from a psychoanalytic perspective. His book is fascinating because it clearly shows how much the food of Mexico is linked to the culture. So much for the postmodern idea that ***architecture*** *is the highest form of a people's expression— he thinks the cultural constructions based on* ***chiles*** *are central to understanding Mexico.*

But, Lomeli has also collected some marvelous and unique recipes including this interesting little one which uses habaneros, radishes and red cabbage. This too is only for the brave, or for those who learn to selectively eat the onions, radishes and the cabbage.

2 regular sized limes

2 habaneros, preferably a green colour

1/2 Spanish onion

1/3 of a small purple leaf cabbage (white is an acceptable option)

2 radishes salt to taste

little bit of water

Chop the onion into fine pieces and place in a colander. Rinse briefly under cold water for a few seconds, and allow to drain. Chop up the habanero into small pieces. Leave the seeds in before chopping for an extra hot salsa, or remove them before chopping if you want a slightly milder version. Chop the cabbage and the radishes into fine pieces. Put all of the chopped ingredients into a salsa bowl. Squeeze the lime juice, add an about an 1/8 cup of water and salt to taste. Pour over the chopped ingredients and mix.

HABANERO, FRUIT AND TOMATO SALSA

1 habanero chile, roasted and chopped

2 tomatoes, peeled and chopped

1 cup each, diced pineapple, papaya and mango

1/4 cup raisins

Combine all of the above ingredients in a very lightly oiled saucepan and heat at a low temperature for about 1/2 hour (or until the tomatoes are cooked). When cooked, the ingredients break down and liquefy, but it thickens after it cools. This is a *hot* 'hot' sauce, but it goes very well with cheese dishes (soufflés) or egg dishes (omelets). Try it with a potato dish like a fritata!

HABANERO AND MANGO SALSA

This habanero salsa combines fruit and veggies. Once again if mango is not available, substitute pineapple, papaya or even mandarins.

2 habaneros, roasted and finely chopped

I large ripe mango, chopped

1/2 cup red onion, finely chopped

1/2 cup each of red and green pepper for extra colour

1/4 cup cilantro, finely chopped

juice of half a lime

dash of dark tequila or mescal

splash of triple sec

Combine ingredients in a glass bowl and keep in refrigerator until ready to use.

Seville Oranges: bitter oranges common to the Yucatan. They are often used to add a hint of bitterness to salsas (much like we use vinegar in salad dressing). Bottled orange juice (*naranja agria*) can be purchased at Latin markets, or add one teaspoon of vinegar to the juice of one orange.

HABANERO MAYONNAISE

That old standby mayonnaise comes to life when spiced with habanero. Here's a recipe inspired by one of Patricia Quintana's books Cuisine of the Water Gods. Jim thinks she is a marvelous cook, and he swears that this has nothing to do with the glamorous photo of her on the cover. This particular cookbook features regional recipes. The habanero mayonnaise hails from Celestun and Chelem in the southern state of Yucatan. These two beach communities are known for local seafood specialties and both have many stands, which serve this tasty topping with crab. Many tourists go to these communities to observe the thousands of wintering flamingos. Note this mayo can be made with either a habanero or serrano chile..

2 cups mayonnaise

1/2 cup plain yogurt

1/2 cup finely chopped red onion

juice of 4 limes

1 fresh habanero (or serrano chile), roasted and finely chopped

2 small cloves garlic, peeled, roasted and ground

1 tbs. minced cilantro

salt to taste

Use a spatula to combine the mayonnaise and yogurt in a medium bowl. Stir in the red onion, lime juice, chile, garlic, cilantro, and salt. Refrigerate for 2 hours.

Habanero salsas are Yucatan favorites, and they go especially well with any pork dish or with chicken.

• All are very, very, very, very, very, very hot.

• For a sweeter touch, add fruit or raisins to any one of these salsas (mango, orange, and papaya). They are also complemented by chopped pineapple or mandarin oranges.

My Notes About Snappies

Stuffers

Meet the stuffers- the poblano, New Mexico and Anaheim chiles. We call these fresh chiles "the stuffers" because they're primarily used as a casing for a variety of fillings. You'll recognize the long green New Mexico chile- it's been widely available for years in parts of Canada and the USA. But the dark green, odd-shaped poblano has just recently become available in supermarkets outside Mexico and the southwestern US. Both of these stuffers are relatively mild. Read on!

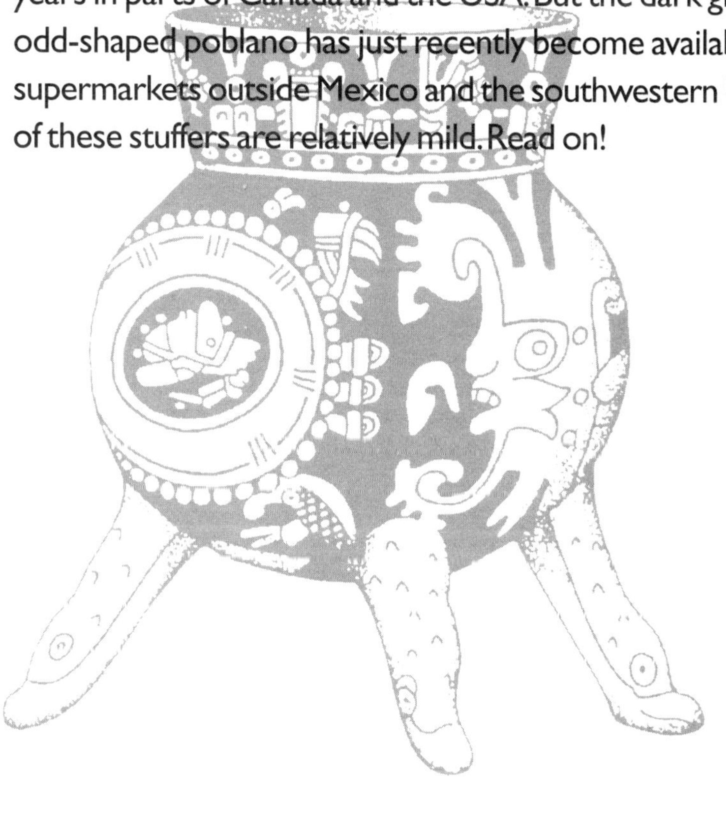

Poblanos, New Mexico and Anaheim Chiles

The poblano and New Mexico chiles are pictured below and you can see how their shapes are different. They also have distinctive flavours even though they are frequently substituted for each other.

Poblanos, Anaheims, and serranos

You might recognize the *poblano* as the chile in the famous stuffed dish "*Chiles En Nogada*". This delightfully rich concoction was featured in the film "*Like Water For Chocolate*"— that colourful platter of stuffed deep green poblano chiles, topped with a white walnut cream sauce and bright red pomegranate seeds.

New Mexico, Anaheim and *poblano* chiles are relatively mild and are used a little like bell peppers except that they are roasted and peeled first. And they have lots more flavour! They're easily stuffed, or added to vegetable dishes. We love them sliced into strips, called '*rajas*', which are fried with onions, potatoes and other vegetables to make a hash. *Rajas* are used as a filling for tortillas or as a tasty topping for meats, fish, sandwiches and salads. And, we also add them to soups.

Poblanos, New Mexico and Anaheim *Salsas*

Although usually not the chile of choice for *fresh salsas*, there are some that feature the New Mexico, the Anaheim or the poblano chile pepper. These *fresh* chiles are occasionally added to other hotter chile peppers to make salsas with extra substance, colour and flavour. Poblanos are especially wonderful when used in combination with fruit and raisins; New Mexico and Anaheim chiles are best in tomato based mixtures, or as a complement to the unique flavour of tomatillos.

Stuffing Poblanos and New Mexico Chiles

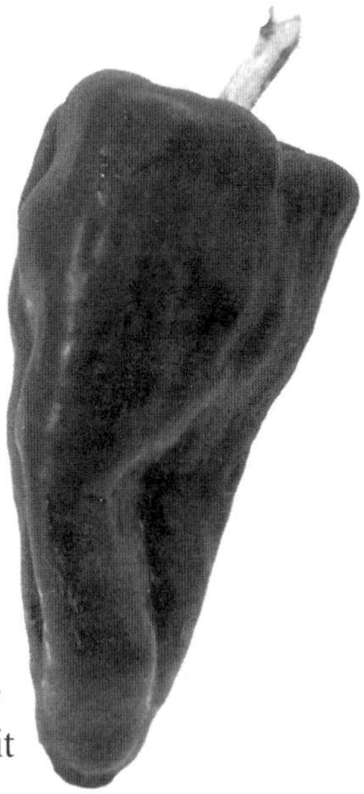

First and foremost, we recommend you *stuff* New Mexico, Anaheim and poblano chiles. In fact, in Sinaloa, Mexico supermarkets the poblano chile is actually labeled *'chile para rellenar'* (chile for stuffing). The filling can be corn, squash, beans, cheese or any number of simple or spicy meat and fish mixtures. The possibilities are endless! Try our suggested recipes and then create your own special fillings. The Spanish name for stuffing is *relleno*, and of course *chiles rellenos* are familiar to almost everyone.

In their fresh form, these types of chiles are extremely versatile. There are so many wonderful recipes based on these *varieties of chile* that they certainly must qualify for some category of MVP award. North of the Rio Grande the most valuable chile is the New Mexico or Anaheim, but south of the border it is definitely the poblano.

And as we'll eventually tell you, they're both incomparable in *dried* versions— and, both are key components of *smooth cooked salsas*. We guarantee that you'll come to appreciate the amazing gastronomic value of these chiles. But let's not get too far ahead of ourselves, and let's wait to talk more about *dried poblanos, dried New Mexico* and *dried Anaheims* later!

Roasting Poblanos on Grill

The New Mexico and Anaheim Chiles

We became very familiar with this type of chile when we lived in Southern Arizona. In fact, an Anaheim was the *first* chile we ate. The New Mexico and Anaheim chiles are most frequently used in *chiles rellenos* but they are also widely used as a condiment. We especially enjoy strips of this chile layered on a crispy *tostada*— made with those huge paper thin flour tortillas of Southern Arizona. And, of course, they're also the main ingredient in *chile verde*, a popular Southern Arizona and New Mexico dish of meat, chiles and onions. In the Mexican State of Sinaloa, Anaheim chiles are just thrown on a barbecue beside the meat dish, and party-goers take a roasted chile when they retrieve their meat. Each person *finger* peels their own Anaheim chile and tears it into strips to eat, or to add to a tortilla with their barbecued meat.

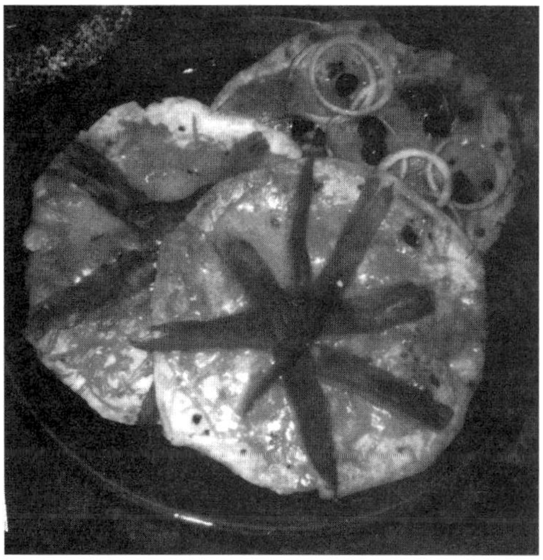

A Cheese Tostada with strips of roasted Anaheim chiles

Indeed, this long green chile is probably the most common ingredient in *borderland* Mexican-American meals.

For many years, the New Mexico/Anaheim chile, along with the jalapeño, has been available in the produce section of major supermarkets in Canada and the US. You'll recognize an Anaheim chile from the pictures we've included here, and all New Mexico chiles have basically the same shape. But, New Mexico chiles do vary in size and have a wider range of colours from a bright lime or yellow green to a deep shiny green. It's also possible to find them in a bright red stage during the fall harvest. The New Mexico chile also varies widely in size, but they are usually about 6-10 inches long (15-25 cm), are relatively fleshy and have a pleasant alkaline taste.

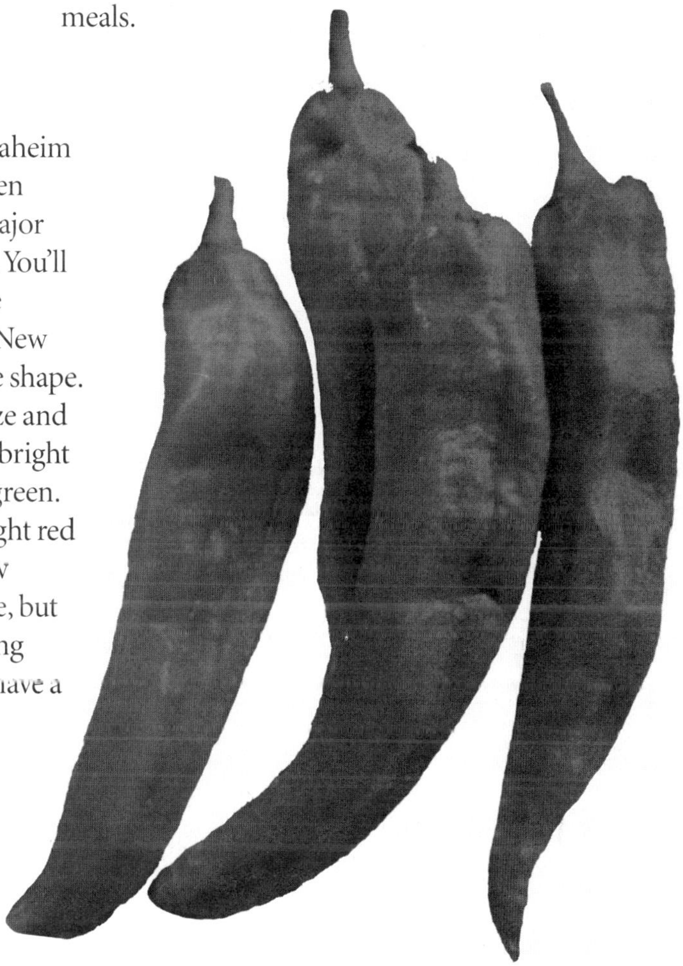

Let's decide on a name

There is much confusion about the name and origin of this chile. Some say it originated in New Mexico and that it was transported to California. Others claim the opposite is true! The most vocal claims come from the State of New Mexico where they insist that an Anaheim chile is simply one member of a *general family* of New Mexico chile peppers . There is big money in marketing chiles with specific qualities (e.g. *size, heat level, thick flesh, thin skin*) and the name argument is partly fueled by a desire to protect specific strains for commercial reasons.

But, the long green chile pepper *is* the state vegetable of New Mexico and has become a State *icon* in its ripened red form. Furthermore, American research on chile peppers is concentrated in New Mexico, and an important Chile Research Institute is located at New Mexico State University. In addition to having a *New Mexico* or *Anaheim* label, the long green chile is sometimes called *California chile*, *stuffing chile*, or simply referred to as *long green chile*. Whatever name you see, any fresh long green chile pepper is used in the same way. In this book, we've decided to use the name *New Mexico chile* to describe any USA version of the fresh long green chile. With apologies to folks in Anaheim— you can brag about Disneyland or Knotts Berry Farm instead!

New Mexico State varieties

New Mexico State chile growers are protective of their product and they always label their chiles to indicate origin. Botanically, they have developedseveral *sub-varieties* and use different names which acknowledge the subtle differences in size, heat level and flavour: *Big Jim* is large, mild and perfect for stuffing; *Sandia* is hotter (more picante) and regularly used in a dried form for making a delicious red sauce; the *Chimayo* comes from a town of this name near Santa Fe, New Mexico and is sweeter and commonly dried and ground into chile powder; the famous *Hatch* chile comes from Hatch, New Mexico and has a deserved reputation as being the best for chile stews and rellenos.

But you'll hardly ever have the opportunity to worry about selecting among different varieties— the long green chiles in local supermarkets are *hardly ever* labeled with specific names. In fact, most come from California or from the States of Colima or Nayarit in Mexico. Occasionally someone ships them directly from Arizona or New Mexico. If the *place of origin* is not indicated, ask your produce manager where they're from (some may even know or be able to produce a shipping box).

The *Big Jim* variety was originally developed for the canning industry.

This extra long, thick fleshed chile was developed so machines could chop tops and tips off chiles and still leave peppers which fit into standardized tins.

Unfortunately, much of the chile pepper was also discarded.

At Fall fiestas in the southwest, sacks of freshly harvested chiles are flame roasted in bulk. They use a custom designed roasting barrel that is hand turned on a roasting hand-crank. The barrel is made of heavy duty mesh with a handle at one end for rotating. A hot gas burner is fired up underneath the barrel filled with chiles. *(see page 24)* *As it rotates the chiles pass through the direct flame. Once roasted they're dumped onto a tray and then easily hand peeled. The aroma created by this technique in incomparable— a uniquely southwestern sensation— right up there with mesquite barbecues, sizzling tortillas and desert rain.*

The long green fresh chile should also be familiar to you in the mature and dried version. Dried red chile strings or *ristras* are a common sight throughout the southwestern United States and are simply air-dried green chiles. *Fresh chiles* are tied on a string and placed in the sun to dry. Many Mexican-American families keep one or two in order to have a year-round supply of ingredients for smooth salsas (see page 105)

Chile Harvest

There's nothing like a chile harvest fiesta. Sacks of freshly picked chiles are trucked into town, thrown into huge cylindrical wire roasters and rotated over a red-hot flame. Blistered and peeling, the chiles are sliced into strips and handed to eager recipients. It's a complete sensual experience— the sight, sound and smell of roasting chiles— and *the taste*! All to the sounds of mariachi music and salsa rythms!

One of our favorite fiestas, *La Fiesta de Los Chiles*, is a Fall event (usually the 3rd week in October) in Tucson Arizona at the Botanical Gardens. This lively fair celebrates the harvest with music, food, and drink— and it features the freshly picked chiles of Benito Gutierrez. On his farm near McNeal, Arizona, Señor Gutierrez grows New Mexico chile peppers by the acre. Because there is such a demand for the *New Mexico variety*, the companies based in New Mexico must purchase chile peppers which are grown elsewhere with seeds provided by the New Mexico growers. For information about fiestas you can search the internet or refer to our resource section on page 181. Specifically, look for Fall events in Hatch New Mexico or in Chimayo New Mexico.

Availability and Substitution

There is absolutely no substitute for a fresh New Mexico chile! However when fresh ones are not available or there is no time to roast and peel— the next best thing is the *canned* version. And if you go with canned, buy *whole* chiles rather than *diced* chiles. Large cans of green chiles are widely available throughout the southwestern USA. These large cans may be difficult to find in other parts of the United States and Canada— but you can check out your local Latino store to see if they carry this product. They are often sold, in diced form in very small cans at very large prices. Buy a big can even if a recipe calls for just a few; place the unused chiles in a sealed plastic container and put it in your freezer.

From the field to the Festival. Scenes from Tucson Chile Harvest Festival

The Poblano

With its shiny surface, deep green colour and sensuous shape, the poblano is without doubt one of the most seductive chiles. In fact, some photographers seem to specialize in taking exotic pictures of it. Poblanos have become our chile of choice for Mexican and southwestern cooking. The flavour is unique— mellow, but complex and earthy. Now widely available north of the the Rio Grande, it looks a bit like a bell pepper. However, it has different and more sophisticated uses than the simple bell pepper. Poblanos are pungent with a hint of a bite, but are not used for their "picante" quality. The poblano (and its dried red version the ancho) is the most popular chile in Mexico. In fact, it accounts for 1/5 of all chiles consumed there.

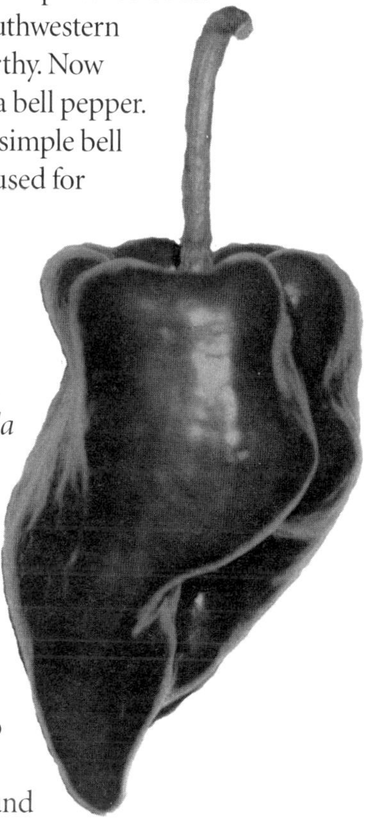

The poblano is named after the city of Puebla in Mexico. In some places the poblano is mysteriously called something else. For example, in Southern California it's routinely called a *pasilla* (or *pascilla*)— a name many supermarkets use when they've obtained these chiles from a specific region of Southern California.

More name confusion:

This is confusing because there is a *pasilla chile*, which is quite different (see our discussion on page 118). To confuse matters more, in some parts of California both the fresh green poblano and its dried version are called an *ancho* chile. In Mexico, the *ancho* is always the *dried version of a fresh poblano chile pepper*, and they even use unique names for anchos dependent on the colour. For instance, if very dark they're called *negro* or *mulato*. If deep brown, they're called *chocolato*. So, it can get quite confusing. But just think— if we insisted on calling every apple type by its unique name or colour it would also be confusing.

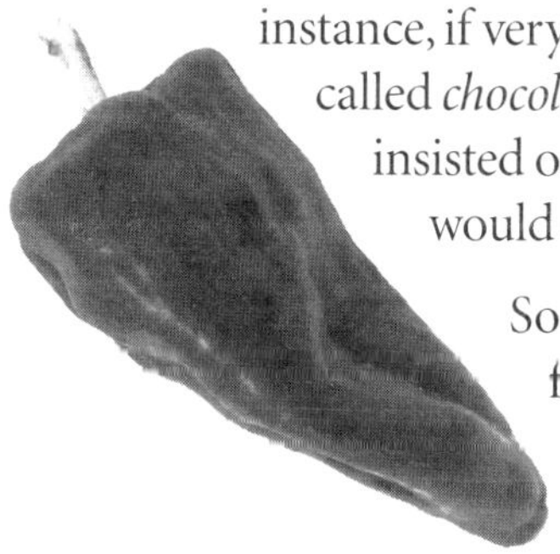

So let's talk about these wonderful chiles as we do apples and focus on the *general name*. When you see a beautiful green chile, shaped somewhat like a bell pepper but darker, longer and more triangular it's a poblano.

Rio Bravo: Mexicans refer to the Rio Grande as the Rio Bravo.

Poblano Use

Although the poblano is most often *stuffed*, it can be used in other ways as well. In fact, *mole poblano*, considered by many to be the quintessential Mexican dish, is made with the dried version of the poblano—the *ancho*. It's called mole poblano because it's believed to have been created in the beautiful city of Puebla in the convent of Santa Rosa.

As the story goes, Sor Andrea del Asuncion, a Dominican nun in charge of the fantastic kitchen at Santa Rosa, whipped up a *mole poblano* for an unexpected important guest— the Viceregal Archbishop. Panic stricken after discovering the shortage of basic food stuffs in her kitchen, she rounded up everything she could get her hands on— dried chiles, nuts, fruits, seasonings, chocolate, and puréed them all together into a thick sauce in which she stewed a turkey. Who cares whether this story is truth or fable— *it's a good tale* and *mole poblano* is a winner! It is a rich, complex sauce— utterly unique and delicious. And it couldn't exist without the poblano chile.

The Convent of Santa Rosa is now a museum in Puebla. The museum has a permanent exhibit— a marvelous collection of popular arts. The kitchen, where mole poblano is reputed to have been created, is considered one of the most beautiful in the country. And, it's something to see!

The beautiful kitchen at Santa Rosa Convent

Mole Poblano is a featured dish at many restaurants in Puebla. One of the best versions of this marvelous concoction is served at a great little restaurant called the Fonda Santa Clara.

Mole simply means a *'mixture'* as in the familiar 'guacamole, (a mixture of aguacate or avocado, tomatoes and chile)

Scenes from the Fonda Santa Clara in Puebla.
There is also one in Mexico City.

The poblano chile can also be cut into strips (*rajas*) and fried with onions, potatoes or eggs, used as a simple relish on top of salads, mixed with meats, dropped into soups, or used in the famous *chile con queso*. Poblanos can also be added to salsas for extra flavour and colouring, and they are particularly tasty in a fruit salsa.

Poblanos are for stuffing…

But for now, we'll focus on the *whole fresh poblano*, which is most often *stuffed*. It is roasted, peeled, deseeded and deveined before use. Just follow the directions we provided for roasting and peeling chiles (see page 17).

Because the New Mexico chile and the poblano are both *stuffers*, they are often used interchangeably. So, we've decided to present the recipes for both types of chiles together. Feel free to make a substitution depending on which fresh chile you find at the market.

There's a reason for the colours of Chiles En Nogada. It was first prepared to celebrate Mexican Independence Day (September 15) and the green, red and white are the colours of the Mexican flag. But this rich, complex specialty from the Puebla area can be enjoyed anytime. In Mexico, they say "Que Chula Es Puebla!", and this dish is truly as pretty as the city.

Halloween Jack O'Lantern using fresh and dried chiles.

THE STUFFER RECIPES: Poblanos and New Mexico Chiles

Stuffed chiles or *chiles rellenos* are not easy to make— but they're definitely worth the effort. We provide some shortcuts and tricks to simplify the task and reduce risk of failure.

During Lent in Mexico (*Cuaresma*), the poblano is the *shell* for many creative non-meat stuffings. These meals contradict the idea that Lenten dishes have to be boring. The stuffings are limited only by the imagination— and in fact many recipe books simply say add a *picadillo*— that is any type of 'hash mixture'.

We've gathered a few of our favorite basic stuffed recipes (*relleno* is Spanish for stuffed) and describe them in the next few pages. With most *rellenos*, you can use *either* a poblano or a New Mexico chile. However, do remember that each chile adds a distinct flavour— so try both and decide which you prefer. Of course some recipes are traditionally poblano and others are uniquely New Mexico chile. We'll tell you when this is the case.

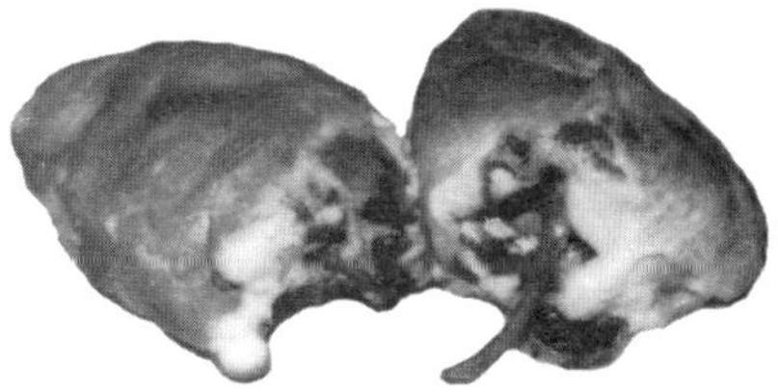

Before and after you stuff

There are several ways to *prepare* the chile peppers for stuffing and there are several ways to cook them *after* they're stuffed. *Chiles rellenos* might be served hot or cold, *with or without* a covering sauce, *battered or plain, baked or fried*— all of these options depending on the filling and particular tastes. But no matter what type of *rellenos* you prepare, here's how to start.

Preparing Chiles for Rellenos

For the fullest flavour, roast New Mexico chiles and poblanos using the instructions on page 17 . They are always roasted, and bagged for about 20 minutes before peeling the outer skin. Remove as much of the outer skin as carefully as possible without tearing the juicy underlying flesh. After peeling, make a small slit in the side and near the top of the chile. Experiment, and try to make the cut very small. Later, if it is necessary you can make the slit a little bigger. But work gingerly when removing the seeds and veins from the small slit in the chile. We use a sharp fruit knife with a fine tip and flexible blade for deveining and deseeding— but any sharp and flexible paring knife works well. Once the seeds have been removed, rinse the chile gently in a light stream of cool water and set on a paper towel to dry. The chile is now ready for stuffing.

An alternative method— Parboiling

We've tried another, less challenging way to soften up chiles for stuffing! If we have older chiles, or thick skinned chiles, we've prepared a deep bath of boiling water and drop chiles into the bath for two or three minutes. When treated this way, the chiles keep their form and they don't have to be peeled. The seeds and veins can be removed before *or* after boiling. Of course there is a *big trade off.* Parboiled chiles are not as flavourful— but with some chiles it is the best option.

An observation about stuffing jalapeños

Lately, it is popular to make little hors d'oevres with stuffed *jalapeños*. Many of the fillings we describe below work well with jalapeños. However, the preparation for stuffing jalapeños is a little different than the preparation for poblanos or New Mexico green chiles.

We think that it is best to always use a parboiling technique when preparing the picante jalapeño. A boiling water bath is easier to manage than roasting, and besides the hot water reduces some of the heat in the jalapeño if you prefer less bite.

After stuffing poblanos and New Mexico chiles

Once you have skinned or parboiled the chile, fill the chile with your choice of stuffing . Then the stuffed chile can be *battered* and *fried* using one of the following techniques on the next page.

RELLENOS BATTER NUMBER ONE

Carefully separate 3 eggs. Beat the egg whites until they are stiff. Next, lightly beat the egg yolks and then fold them into the stiffened white mixture. To assemble the rellenos, roll the individual chile in plain white flour and then dip into the beaten egg mixture.

Optional: you can add a little bit of baking powder to the flour mixture.

You fry the coated chile in a thin layer of hot oil until the coating puffs up and is golden brown. Remove the stuffed chile from the oil and drain it on paper towels. Or, once you become confident handling the chiles, drop a large serving-spoon of the egg mixture into the hot oil and then quickly plop a stuffed chile pepper right on top of the batter while it is frying. When you do this, use a spatula to *flip* some of the egg mixture on top of the chile and turn the whole mixture over once it has cooked on the bottom side.

3 eggs, separated
white flour
baking powder *(optional)*

RELLENOS BATTER NUMBER TWO

Here's an easier, and quicker way to batter stuffed chiles as suggested by Jackie McMahon in her book Chiles Red and Green.

Prepare 2 separate platters— one with a layer of flour and the other with a thin pool of buttermilk. *Optional:* add a few spices like ground cumin to the flour, and you can also add a little bit (1/4 tsp.) of baking powder to the flour.

First, roll the stuffed chile in the flour and then quickly drag it through the buttermilk. The dredged chile goes one more time into the flour mixture to provide a thicker coating. Of course, this chile and batter is fried in hot oil as described above in batter number one. Try this easy alternative and see what you think! It's nice and crispy but perhaps not as tasty as the egg batter version.

But of course, it's cholesterol reduced!

flour
buttermilk
ground cumin
baking powder
oil for frying

Preparation Tips

Try to leave the stems intact— whole stuffed chile peppers look great.

To Parboil

- Wash chiles and place in a cooking pot.
- Cover with water and boil until colour changes and flesh softens.
- Remove, slit the side *just enough* to scrape out seeds and veins. The chile is now ready for stuffing.

Frying Rellenos in Oil

- It's a good idea to use an oil like canola or peanut oil. These tolerate higher temperatures well and don't break down as easily.
- Pour about an 1/8" to 1/4" of oil into the fry pan and turn it up to about medium high. Don't let the oil get so hot that it smokes.
- Be careful when you drop in the first coated chile, because the oil may splatter.
- If the chile cooks too quickly, then turn down the temperature of the oil a slight amount. The oil has to be hot enough to quickly cook the battered chile.

North Americans (outside Mexico) are probably most familiar with the battered, cheese stuffed relleno. However in Mexico many rellenos are often served 'naked'. They are just as good, easier to make and lower in fat. It's up to you whether you 'batter' or not and whether you bake or fry. And, as you can see from the following recipes, stuffed rellenos are excellent as a cold dish.

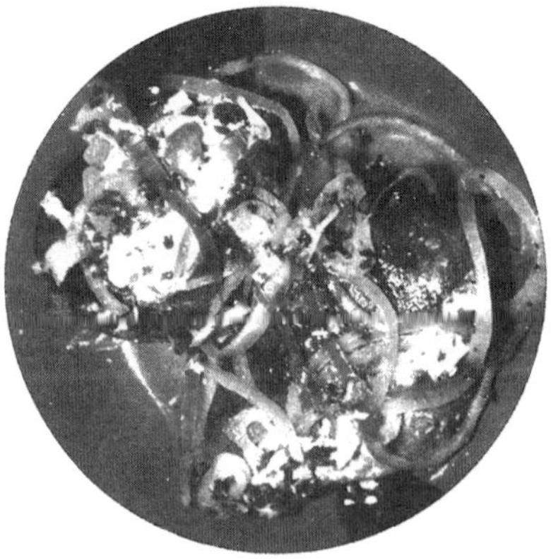

These poblanos were roasted, peeled, and cleaned. They were then lightly fried and stuffed with a tuna, potatoes and onion mixture. They were chilled, covered with red onion slices and served cold.

Stuffer recipes.

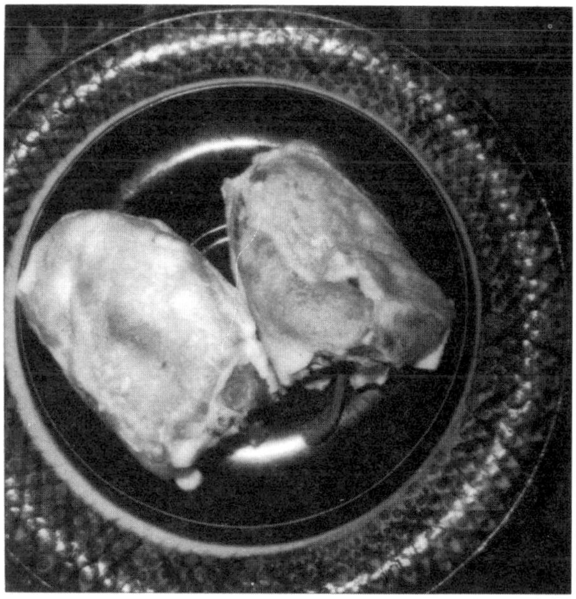

RELLENOS CLASSICO!

Let's start with those classic chiles rellenos stuffed with cheese, battered and then pan fried. Use either the New Mexico chile or the poblano with your choice of cheese. Unfortunately, the wonderful cheese from Mexico is not widely available— yet. As a rule of thumb we suggest using a Monterey jack or farmers cheese with the poblano and a soft cheddar or a colby with the New Mexico chile. Chiles rellenos should be prepared just before serving, which makes this a difficult dish for special dinners. But you can prepare and stuff the chiles ahead of time and then store them covered in the refrigerator for several hours. Or, try the chiles rellenos casserole recipe that follows the classico. It's definitely not the same, but a very good alternative.

6 large poblano or New Mexico chiles— roasted, peeled, seeded and deveined with the stems left on.

1/2 lb. of farmers, colby or longhorn cheese cut into long strips

3 eggs separated

flour

oil for frying

Carefully slit each chile with a lengthwise cut and fill each one with strips of cheese. Beat the egg whites until stiff; beat egg yolks gently with fork. Add the yolks back into the white mixture. Roll the chiles in flour. Heat the oil in skillet and drop spoonful of egg mixture onto pan. (or dip each stuffed chile in egg mixture and then place in pan). Place one chile into the centre and spoon more egg mixture over it to cover. Fry until a golden colour on all sides. Remove from oil and place on paper towel.

These can be served *straight from the frying pan* with a fresh salsa, or topped with the quickie hot tomato sauce below.

Quickie Tomato Sauce for Rellenos

oil

4 cloves of garlic, peeled

1/2 onion chopped

1 can cooked plum tomatoes

3 cups chicken broth

Heat oil in large fry pan. Sauté the garlic and onion. Add a can of cooked tomatoes with 3 cups of chicken broth. Simmer for 10 minutes or longer. Store any leftover in the fridge or freezer.

CHILES RELLENOS— THE CASSEROLE

Here's the chile relleno casserole we mentioned earlier. Definitely not the real thing but not a bad alternative if you have guests and want to avoid the fuss, bother and possible embarrassment of stuffing chiles in front of a live audience.

6 New Mexico or poblano chiles, roasted, peeled, deseeded and deveined.

1/2 lb. of farmers, Monterey jack, colby or cheddar cheese cut into strips

3 eggs, separated

1/4 cup flour

Stuff the chiles with cheese. Beat the egg whites until stiff. Sift the flour and fold it into egg whites. Beat the egg yolks and fold into flour—egg white mixture. Place half of the egg and flour mixture into a lightly greased casserole dish. Then place stuffed chiles on top. Cover the chiles with the remaining egg and flour mixture. Bake at 400ºF until brown on top (about 20-30 minutes). Serve with or without quickie tomato sauce from the previous page.

CHILES RELLENOS WITH SHRIMP AND CHIPOTLE MAYO

Now here are two chile relleno recipes that use fish or shrimp as the stuffing. One dish is served hot, the other cold. Both are unbreaded and the perfect meal— low in fat, high in flavour.

8 fresh poblano or New Mexico chiles–roasted, peeled, seeded and deveined
1 lb. of cooked and peeled shrimp
6 green onions, chopped
cilantro
variety of salsas

<u>Chipotle Mayo</u>

1/2 cup mayo

1/2 cup sour cream or yogurt

1 canned chipotle in adobo, chopped (see page 136)

Once chiles are peeled, seeded and deveined, slit them lengthwise leaving on the stem. Mix shrimp and onions and carefully spoon into each chile. Barbecue or heat in oven until mixture is hot.

Prepare the mayo by mixing all ingredients and refrigerating (see page 133 for more information about *chipotles)*. The small cans have about 6 individual chiles. Use only 1 to start. Freeze the others. Serve the chiles rellenos with this chipotle mayo *and* an assortment of condiments.

OPTION: Remember the Shrimp Supreme from Escuinapa on page 41. It is a fantastic filling for this dish.

CHILES STUFFED WITH TUNA

This next recipe, from the Mexican state of Guerrero, is served cold and is one of our favorites. It's light and yet is substantial enough to be a main dish. It is best made with poblano chiles but Anaheims substitute in a pinch. In Mexico City they often substitute a pickled cuaresmeño (a very large jalapeño) which makes the recipe a tad spicier. Serve with beans, tortillas, or rolls. It is excellent accompanied by a light soup.

6 chile poblanos (or 6 New Mexico—roasted, peeled, seeded and deveined

2 tsp. of vinegar

1 tbs. of oil clove of garlic

dash of oregano

one small onion chopped

1/4 cup of water

Filling

2 potatoes, cooked and cubed

1 can white tuna fish

1/4 small onion chopped

pinch of cumin seed

1 tsp. hot mustard

2 tbs. of mayo or to taste

Heat the oil in pan and sauté the cleaned chiles briefly until they are softened. Remove and place on a plate for stuffing. Next, add the garlic, oregano, onion, water and vinegar to the pan. Cook on medium heat for about 10 minutes. Remove the vegetables and save liquid.

Prepare filling by combining all ingredients. Fill each chile with tuna mixture and cover with the cooking liquid from the pan. Refrigerate for several hours before serving.

Relleno Variations

- For a non–egg batter, roll in flour, then buttermilk, and then flour again and fry.
- For a low fat alternative, skip the batter and the frying and bake the stuffed chiles in the quickie tomato sauce on page 77.
- Before stuffing,— parboil chiles instead of roasting them.
- Serve battered chiles with a variety of condiments (chopped onions, cilantro, oregano for sprinkling) rather than with the quickie tomato sauce.
- We suggest a tomato-chipotle salsa (page 138) or an ancho-tomatillo (page 116).
- It is also good with a plain yogourt topping, or with a mixture of 1/2 sour cream and 1/2 whipping cream.

Chiles rellenos are perfect for a vegetarian diet. Here are a couple of vegetarian recipes to begin. But remember—anything goes with stuffers! Experiment with other fillings such as rice pilafs, refried beans (black or pinto), tomatoes and onions, potatoes and cheese. Nuts add texture and nutrition!

CHILES RELLENOS CON MAIZ

In this next recipe the chiles are stuffed with a corn filling and are baked— always the low fat option with chile rellenos.

10 fresh poblano or New Mexico chiles–roasted, peeled, deseeded and deveined

Filling

1 red onion, chopped

1/2 green bell pepper, chopped

2 tbs. oil 1 tbs. oregano

1 tsp. cumin

4 cups corn kernels (frozen, canned, fresh)

1/2 cup light sour cream

1/2 cup chopped nuts (pecans or walnuts)

1 lb. jack cheese cut into long, thin slices.

Slit the roasted and peeled chiles lengthwise. Remove seeds and veins. Prepare filling as follows: Heat oil in pan. Sauté onion and green pepper. Add corn, oregano and cumin and stir briefly. Remove from heat and add sour cream and nuts. Arrange chiles on a baking pan and fill each with the corn mixture adding several slices of cheese to each.

Bake in 400°F oven until lightly brown. Remove and serve with choice of fresh or cooked salsas.

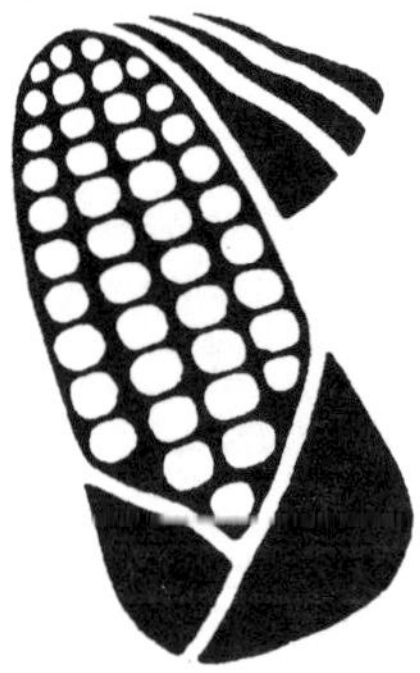

CHILES RELLENOS FRIOS CON GUACAMOLE
(Cold fire-roasted long green chiles stuffed with guacamole)

This recipe is similar to one described in a favourite, but delightfully different, book— The Texas Border Cookbook. This was written by W. Park Kerr and Norma Kerr, the mother-son team who manage the El Paso Chile Company. Their innovative and delicious recipes draw from a solid base of Mexican and southwestern traditions even when they vary from traditional approaches. Use their guacamole filling, described here, or make up your own favorite mixture. These chile rellenos are served cold— salad style.

8 or more large long green chiles

2 tablespoons red wine vinegar

1 teaspoon prepared dijon-style mustard

pinch of salt

1/3 cup olive oil

about 2 cups guacamole

Guacamole Filling

1 cup roughly chopped cilantro

2 fresh jalapeño chiles, roasted, stemmed and chopped

4 large ripe avocados, pitted and peeled

5 or 6 ripe plum tomatoes, halved and diced

1/2 cup diced red onion

1/4 cup mayonnaise
salt to taste

FOR THE GUACAMOLE FILLING: In a blender chop the cilantro and jalapeños. Put the avocados in the blender and pulse to a chunky texture. Add the chopped tomatoes and diced onion and the mayonnaise. Pulse until chunky or smooth (your preference) Season with salt to taste.

FOR THE CHILE RELLENO: Slit the chiles and remove the seeds and veins. Mix the vinegar, mustard and olive oil. Cover the chiles with dressing and let them marinate for at least 1 hour.

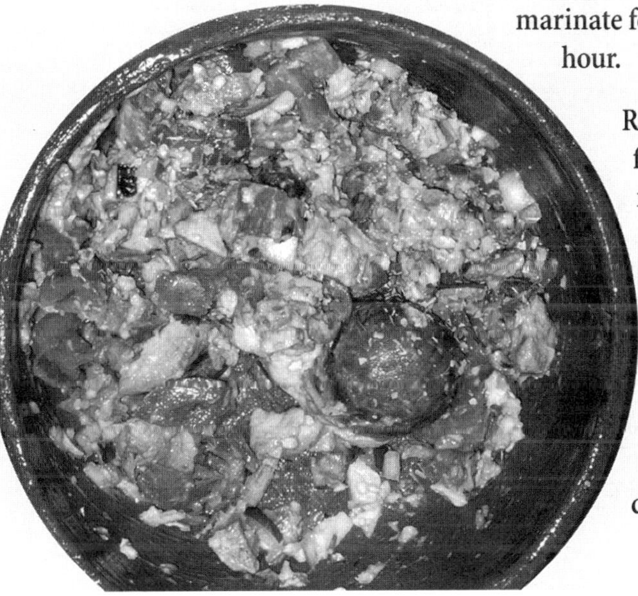

Remove chiles from the marinade and stuff each with a 1/4 cup guacamole. Arrange chiles on platter and drizzle with remaining dressing.

CHILES RELLENOS DE PICADILLO

Here's a classic chiles rellenos dish using poblanos. Do not substitute New Mexico chiles in this recipe! The spicy sweet meat filling is simply called picadillo and this version is absolutely delicious. There are many variations of picadillo mixes. This filling can also be used for the famous Chiles En Nogada described in the next recipe. The rellenos may be battered or left naked. Generally we prefer them without a batter. Chiles Rellenos de Picadillo is a traditional Mexican dish prepared for special occasions like weddings or baptisms. It can be made with beef or pork or a mixture of both meats.

8 poblano chiles–roasted, peeled, deseeded

Picadillo (Beef Filling)

1 lb. lean beef, cooked and shredded or lean ground beef

2 tbs. of oil

1 onion, chopped

1 clove garlic, minced

2 tomatoes, chopped

1 apple, peeled and chopped

1/4 cup seedless raisins

dash of cinnamon, ground cloves and ground cumin

1/2 cup of chicken broth

Sauté the meat in oil until it is browned. Add the onion and garlic, tomatoes, apple, raisins, cinnamon, cloves, cumin and broth. Cook on low heat until everything is softened and has become fairly dry. Slit the chiles lengthwise and fill each with several heaping tablespoons of filling. Serve as is, put on a platter and cover with the simple tomato sauce on page 77.

Tip for Assembly

When the filling has small pieces (e.g. shrimp), it makes sense to use a toothpick to hold the two edges of the chile together. Just overlay the two edges and carefully thread a toothpick along its length.

Machaca: In Arizona, Sonora and Sinaloa, dishes emphasize beef. Machaca is beef soaked in chiles, lime and garlic and sun dried. It is recooked in oil or water with more chiles, onions and tomatoes to make a mouth watering filling.

Chorizo: is a spicy pork sausage used in Mexican cooking. It is most commonly served for breakfast.

The next recipe is much more complex than the others we've included. But it *is* a classic, and it is absolutely delicious. If you don't want to make it, try it when you travel to Mexico or to the larger cities of the American southwest. It is always made with the Poblano Chile and never with the New Mexico chile pepper.

A New Mexico chile version of *Chiles Rellenos* is not as complicated as this recipe for *Chile en Nogada*— a stuffed New Mexico chile typically uses a simple cheese filling.

CHILES EN NOGADA

Chiles en Nogada are familiar if you saw "Like Water for Chocolate". It's a very special dish, usually reserved for special occasions— like Mexican Independence Day (Sept. 15), Cinco de Mayo (May 5 of course), or Christmas. It is complicated to make and we include it here simply because it's one of the best known chile poblano dishes and, with mole poblano— one of the most richly flavoured dishes in all Mexico. Over the years many versions of this dish have sprung up. We suggest you check out Diana Kennedy's version in her classic book "Cuisines of Mexico"— and, if you have a few days with nothing to do you might want to try making her recipe. Or, you can try our simplified version.

6 fresh poblanos– roasted, peeled, seeded, deveined but stems left on

Picadillo: from previous recipe

Cream Sauce
1 cup walnuts
1 cup sour cream
2/3 cup half and half
2 tbs. brandy
2 tsp. sugar
1/2 tsp. ground cinnamon
pomegranate seeds and cilantro for garnish

Carefully slit each chile lengthwise. Fill with the picadillo from the recipe for Chiles Relleno de Picadillo on the previous page. Place the chiles on a baking pan and keep them warm (about 225°F) in oven while you prepare the sauce.

Grind the walnuts in blender or nut grinder. Place the crushed nuts in a bowl and add the remaining ingredients (sour cream, half and half, brandy, sugar and cinnamon). Mix. To serve, place the stuffed chiles on plate and cover with this cream and walnut sauce.

Garnish with pomegranate seeds and cilantro.

Other Ways to Use the Stuffers

RAJAS

We can't discuss poblano and New Mexico chiles without telling you how to make rajas. It's so easy! Rajas simply mean strips and they are pronounced 'rah-haws'. Cut the roasted, peeled chiles lengthways into strips which are about half the width of your little finger. Use them as is, or fry them with onions. These rajas can be used in any number of ways— served as a vegetable accompaniment, as a condiment with meat, added to other vegetables like potatoes ,corn, tomatoes or squash, japanese eggplant, as a topping for salad, soup, or stew, added to sandwiches, tacos or quesadillas as a relish. Rajas add spice and flavour to any dish. The next time you barbecue fresh squash— add a little olive oil and lay on a single raja.

6 poblano or New Mexico chiles– roasted, peeled, deseeded and deveined and cut into strips

3 onions

2 teaspoons cumin

2 tablespoons olive oil

Heat oil in skillet. Slice onions in diagonal strips and place in skillet along with chile strips and cumin. Fry until onion is soft.

Put in a container in the refrigerator, or use immediately as a condiment.

Next, we'll describe a few classic green chile recipes even though they're not exactly stuffers. One of the most popular appetizers with New Mexico green chiles is *Chile Con Queso,* which simply means 'chile with cheese'.

CHILE CON QUESO

This appetizer is from Northern Mexico and is often served at parties in the southwest. There are many variations to this dish—some leave out cream, some use cream cheese, some use tomato sauce, some use extra heavy cream. This is a version that's in-between. It's easy to make and canned green chiles can easily be substituted without affecting the taste. And, yes it's disgustingly fattening. No substitutes allowed!

12 New Mexico chiles– roasted, peeled, deseeded and chopped or 12 canned green chiles

1 tbs. oil

1 onion, chopped

3 tomatoes, chopped

1 cup heavy cream

1 cup shredded colby, cheddar, or Monterey jack

Heat oil and sauté onions. Add chiles and tomatoes and cook about 5 minutes. Add the cream. Cook, stirring until hot. Reduce heat to low and add cheese, stirring until melted. Serve hot in fondue dish with chips, crackers or vegetables.

CHILE VERDE

Here's another classic Mexican dish popular throughout the southwest. It's called chile verde and, once again, there are many versions. This one uses pork but you can substitute beef. You can also add a few jalapeños for more bite.

10 New Mexico green chiles– roasted, peeled, deseeded and deveined (or 10 canned green chiles)

4 lb. boneless pork cut into cubes

2 tbs. oil

1 onion chopped

4 cloves garlic, minced

1 tsp. oregano

1 tsp. cumin

Cover meat with water and boil, and then turn down the heat. Simmer until meat is tender. Drain, add the oil and heat the pan to let the meat brown. Add onion, garlic, tomatoes, chiles and seasonings. Cover and cook 10 minutes more at medium high heat. Reduce the heat and then simmer for 15 minutes. Serve with condiments: cilantro, avocado, sour cream, and warm flour tortillas.

THE BABY T

Here's a delicious recipe created by Mary Lou's sister Kris. Mary Lou and Kris, along with many volunteer friends and relatives, served Baby T's at several festivals in Canada and the US. The Baby T is a small version of the tostada (sometimes called cheese crisps) which we often ate at restaurants in Tucson, Arizona. They use large paper thin flour tortillas crisped in the oven and topped with butter, cheese, chiles, onions, or machaca (dried meat mixture)— or all of the above. We served a miniature version of this at Tucson's Fiesta de Los Chiles—topped with whole, freshly roasted New Mexico chiles from Gutierrez' farm. For the chorizo, you can make your own, or stock up on a dried package mix such as that provided by National Spices in Phoenix, Arizona. It's an excellent product of mixed spices— just add to ground pork, beef, chicken or turkey. We provide a recipe in the dried chile section (page 124) for those who really are adventurous or won't be in Phoenix for the weekend.

12 New Mexico or Anaheim chiles–roasted, peeled, seeded, deveined (or 12 whole canned green chiles)

12 small flour tortillas (4"-5" across)

1 lb. ground turkey chorizo (see page124)

1 cup grated cheddar or colby cheese

Salsa Mexicana (see page 33)

Deep fry tortillas in frying pan, drain them on paper towels. Sprinkle cheese on tortillas. Top with 2 tbs. of turkey chorizo, one whole chile cut into raja strips, and and top with Salsa Mexicana (see page 33) or any other fresh salsa.

NEW MEXICO GREEN CHILE SALSA NUMBER I.

Yes, poblanos and New Mexico chiles are definitely the relleno chiles, but occasionally they are also used in salsas. Here are two examples!

3 New Mexico or Anaheim chiles—roasted, peeled, seeded and deveined (or 3 whole canned green chiles)

2 tbs. oil

1/2 red or white onion, chopped

6 ripe roma tomatoes, diced or 1 cup canned whole tomatoes

1 tbs. vinegar

1/4 cup cilantro, chopped

Heat onion in oil. Stir in chiles and remove from heat. Add tomatoes and vinegar. Refrigerate several hours and add cilantro just before serving.

NEW MEXICO GREEN CHILE SALSA NUMBER II.

And yes, here's another variation! This is a salsa verde that uses the long green chiles (the specific varieties from New Mexico State are a lovely lime green) and tomatillos.

2 fresh New Mexico or Anaheim chiles–roasted, peeled and deveined (or 2 whole canned green chiles)

1/2 lb. tomatillos, prepared as on p. 35

1/4 cup minced fresh cilantro

2 garlic cloves, minced

1/4 lb. onions, chopped

1 tbs. virgin olive oil

2 tsp. vinegar

Drain tomatillos. Put in blender or food processor with remaining ingredients. Blend to desired consistency. Cover and refrigerate.

BEGINNING WITH

Chiles

DRIED CHILES

Selection, Preparation and Storage

Dried chiles are used in one of two ways:

- They're stored whole and later toasted, rehydrated and liquefied with other ingredients to make smooth sauces like enchilada or mole.
- They're crushed into a fine powder which is *either* used to make a extra-smooth sauce *or* made into a dry seasoning.

After drying— chiles acquire an intensity of flavour that's not present in their fresh form. They become fruity, nutty or occasionally sweet. Smaller ones like *chiles de arbol, pequins* or *chiltepins* become significantly hotter and make super seasoners. Larger ones like the *anchos*, or *chipotles* might not add as much heat as the little guys but they increase the complexity of any salsa making it richer, earthier or smokier. In the next chapter, we'll talk about making these sauces and in the chapter after that we'll come back to the seasonings.

If you want to dry your own there are detailed instructions in The Whole Chile Pepper Book. On the internet, instructions are found at http://www.nmsu.edu/~hotchile/chilei4.htm

Fresh New Mexico chiles and the dried chile colorado version

The most widely recognized dried chiles are those in *chile ristras*— those strings of red chiles that are a symbol of southwest harvests . Traditionally, only larger New Mexico chiles were dried for making smooth sauces, but nowadays you also find ristras made of the smaller chiles de arbol. Actually, any chile that's not too fleshy can be dried in this manner and later rehydrated into a red chile paste or crushed and used as a seasoner .

Families would string ristras for each person in the family. In order to get through the winter, a ristra was made to a length 1 1/2 each member's height.

Four basic dried chiles. *Clockwise from the top,*
•chiles chipotles (smoke dried jalapeños)
•chiles de arbol,
•chiles colorados (air dried New Mexico variety),
•dried anchos (air dried poblano chiles).

Chile Powders

Before we talk about preparing *whole* dried chile peppers, we have a word of caution about packaged chile powders! Ground chile powder, in various brand names, has been available for years. But many commercial powders are mixtures of smaller non-identified dried chiles *along with* garlic, oregano and other spices.

McCormicks and Company is a source of chile powder and other spices for southwestern and Mexican Cooking.

Their cinnamon and oregano are the real Mexican version.

Almost everyone has a bottle of chile powder on the spice shelf— especially if they've been to an Asian market. But, before you consider using those commercial chile powders in Mexican cooking for making sauces or creating blends of seasonings— *check the ingredients*. If there are spices besides chiles then look for one *without* those extra ingredients. If one brand doesn't describe the type of chile used to make the powder— then find one that does!

Prepared chile powders commonly use *paprika* or *tabasco* chile peppers which are more pungent than peppers used in Mexican dishes and they're not suitable for producing the smooth sauces of this style of cooking. McCormick's obtains many spices from Mexico— and as a rule of thumb, the unnamed chiles in *McCormick's and Company* packages are probably chiles de arbol, pequins or something similar. These are useful for blending authentic Mexican seasonings but not for making sauces.

The highest quality chile powders use *ground ancho chiles* or the *true Mexican pasilla chile* and these are excellent choices for making smooth sauces. Ancho chile powder is a dark brownish-red colour and is frequently labeled '*puro*'. A true pasilla chile powder is almost black and has a rich earthy smell. Another excellent chile powder without extra ingredients is made from dried *chimayo* chiles from New Mexico. Look for these types of chiles if you want to make authentic sauces, and make sure that you buy in bulk. You will need about 3/4 cup of chile powder to make a sauce for one main dish.

Finding chile powder

But even if you can't find *pure chile* powders, you will always achieve outstanding results with *whole* dried chiles. In fact, sauces are always richer with dried chile peppers— chile powder never captures the intensity of flavour that comes from whole dried peppers!

But packaged chile powder *is* more convenient and always makes a very *smooth* sauce. So if powder is your choice for making smooth sauces, then make sure that you purchase *authentic* or *pure* chile powder in Mexican and Latin American grocery stores. Ask your friends to bring some home when they travel to the southwest USA or Mexico. We don't recommend that you buy a sackfull of the stuff when you do find it— because chile powders eventually become bitter. But you will be able to keep a small container on your spice shelf for a year before you might notice any difference.

These pure chile powders are available by mail order if you can't find them in your home town— or if your friends won't accommodate your request. You can easily obtain several months supply with one mail order. One of our favorite sources is the Santa Cruz Chile and Spice Co. in Tumacacori, Arizona. Other mail order companies will happily send you a supply of pure ground chile powders with no other ingredients added to the precious chile powder.

As a general rule of thumb, the chile powders ground from the *New Mexico reds* are the *cheapest*— and chiles from darker varieties are much more expensive. Ground black pasilla chiles can cost a small fortune. At the back of this book (page 180) we suggest a few places to purchase chiles by mail. Those of you in the electronic age can easily locate many web sites that supply dried chiles and powders.

In many parts of Mexico, salsas are made in a molcajete (volcanic dish) instead of licuadoras (food processors). These salsas have a unique quality not replicated in the electronic kitchen. They are chunkier, grittier, and individual chiles 'pass through the salsa' rather than blending into one overall taste. However, these molcajetes are made from an especially fine quality stone, and have seasoned over a long period of time.

Equipment?

In old Mexico, almost every kitchen still has a traditional *molcajete* which was used to grind chiles and make fresh salsas. This bowl of volcanic rock was the means of crushing dried chiles. However, tradition has given way to the modern age and almost everyone uses a food processor or a blender, and even in Mexican households the molcajete is a decoration. The ubiquitous '*licuadora*' (blender) has become the utensil of choice. We happen to think that one of the greatest inventions is the *mini* food processor, which handles about one cup of ingredients.

Many versions retail for $30 or less. At home, we grind a few small chiles with a wooden mortar and pestle. We have set aside an old coffee grinder specifically for crushing larger amounts of dried spices.

Varieties of powders

Even though we said to look for *pure* chile powders, it's also true that each region in Mexico has a *special blend* which adds other ingredients to plain dried chile. These special powder blends are called *adobos* or *recados*, and they are always within reach on home counter tops as marinades for meats and as seasoners for soups and stews (*guisos* and *guisados*).

A food processor can be used to grind dried chiles and mix a home-made spice mixture named an adobo.

Favorite regional chiles are mixed with spices like cumin or more exotic ingredients like *achiote* (ground *annato* nut) to make these special seasoning mixtures. These dried spices have more body because of ground nuts or seeds— and have more moisture because they contain vinegar or a few drops of a bitter orange juice (from Seville oranges). The most popular of these mixtures are available in dried form or in bouillon style "cubes" in many markets.

These mixtures are used as quick seasonings in soups, broth and to marinate meats just as Asian cooking uses 5 *spice mixture*, or East Indian cooking uses curry powders and *garam masalas*. In

Adobo: a mixture of various dried spices. There are many regional variations, but many contain cumin, garlic, cloves, cinnamon and regional chiles.
Recado: a mixture of various dried spices which is usually softened with vinegar or a sour fruit liquid. This is the name for a spice mixture in the Yucatan region.
Achiote: An orange—red mixture of spices from the Yucatan. It obtains its red colour from the ground annato nut, and it also has chiles and a sour orange liquid (usually from Seville oranges)

most parts of North and Central Mexico, the mixture is called an *adobo* and dishes cooked with it have the adjective *adobado* as part of their name. In the Yucatán, they call this mixture a *recado* and it inevitably includes ground *annato* and a sour-fruit liquid . Yucatán recados are a beautiful orange-red, and add a unique colour and delicate flavour to seafood, chicken and pork dishes. American chef Reed Hearon wrote an entire book about Yucatán recados (La Parilla: the Mexican Grill) and his contribution is included in our list of recommended books.

Selecting Whole Dried Chiles

In Mexico, people walk out their door and stroll to a neighborhood market to get a supply of dried or fresh chiles. In Mexico City, tent markets (*mercados en rueda* or 'markets on wheels') appear magically 2 days a week in almost all neighborhoods.

Big and small supermarkets in southwestern and borderland American cities have entire shelves of *pre-packaged* whole dry chiles of every type.

However, the further one travels north of the Rio Grande the fewer the options and the higher the prices. But it is possible to buy whole dried chiles almost everywhere, and the prices are actually reasonable. To our great surprise, we found prepackaged high quality dried anchos in several mega-markets of Western Canada.

When you see whole dried chiles, especially dried anchos or chipotles— snap them up and take them home. They keep indefinitely in jars or in tightly sealed plastic freezer bags. It is best to put them in a container in order to keep them free of bugs and dust.

When buying large dried chiles, either packaged or loose, look for deep-red or a reddish-chocolate colour. If you hold them to the light and it's translucent— buy them at any price. Check that any chile is free of brown spots or mold, which might indicate bugs. Also, choose chiles that have been recently dried! These are always more flexible, aromatic and softer than older chiles.

A high quality ancho chile is almost golden and is translucent. Lower grade qualities are generally green-black and opaque.

Storing dried chiles

As we said, dried chiles keep almost indefinitely when stored properly. Put them in a cool, dry place after they are packed whole in tightly sealed jars. Whole dried chiles keep indefinitely in the freezer if they are in a tightly closed plastic bag. If you dragged a ristra home, hang it in a cool and dry spot and periodically turn it so that the dust doesn't all settle on one side.

In Mexico chiles are left on the plant to dry or they're just laid on the ground. In the southwestern US, hanging the chile ristras to dry is a functional as well as decorative approach but of course this is labour intensive.

Roasting: Fresh chiles are usually roasted using one of the techniques described earlier.
Toasting: The larger dried chiles are also cooked, but this process is often referred to as toasting.

Cooking with Dried Chiles

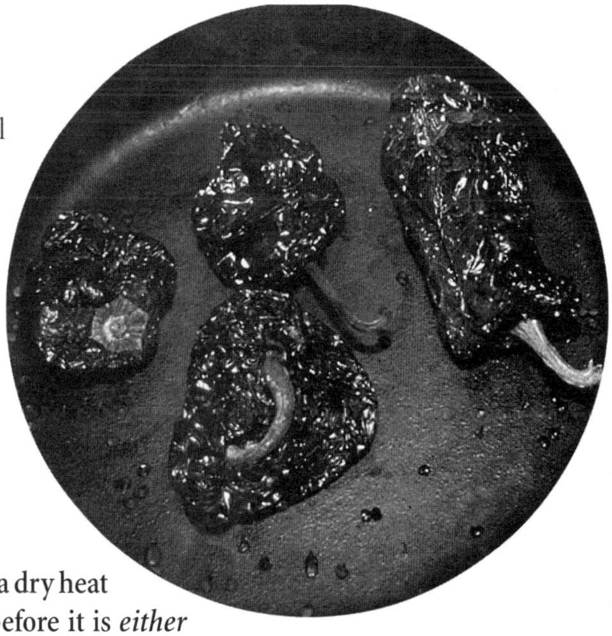

Larger whole dried chiles gain a great deal of flavour if they are cooked before they are used. It's possible to toast smaller chiles but it's not always done. Preparing dried chiles is only a little more complicated than roasting fresh ones— and there really are no special skills or equipment involved. All those tips that we gave you about handling fresh chiles also apply to whole dried chiles.

Dried chiles are cooked to release aromatic oils. This is done in two very different ways:

- **The most common method uses a dry heat technique to *warm up the chile* before it is *either* ground up *or* rehydrated in a liquid.**
- **The other technique uses hot oil to *poach* a chile before it is dropped into a liquid for rehydration.**

Heating fresh chiles on a comal is called *roasting.*

This same process for dried chiles is called *toasting.*

Toast dried chiles— you'll have fuller, more complex flavours.

Toasting Dried Chiles

Some recipes call for rehydrating a whole dried chile by simply covering it with a hot liquid. However, toasting releases wonderful flavours and oils and *we highly recommend that you do this*. In fact, the advantage of whole dried chiles over powders is this additional flavour!

Toasting can be done in a fry pan, in the oven, or over a hot grill. First, wipe the surface of the dried chile with a slightly damp cloth or paper towel to remove any dust or dirt. (chile ristras hanging in your living room get pretty dusty). Heat the fry pan until it's moderately hot. The pan is hot ready if you sprinkle a tiny bit of water on it and it collects into little drops and evaporates. Place the chiles on this hot surface, and watch them closely. Turn them often until they're toasted on all sides.

Although light toasting usually releases the flavours,— some regional Mexican dishes toast until the chiles are dark and blackened.

Experiment by roasting for shorter or longer time periods.

When toasting, a chile puffs up, expands and releases a tantalizing aroma. In the case of dried anchos, it almost appears that they are springing back to life because of this 'puffing' effect.

But do be careful! Dried chiles burn very quickly and can turn into a blackened crisp before you know it. Take extra care to avoid the fumes— since volatile capsaicin is released in the vapours and you can burn your eyes or your face. When the chile is toasted on all sides and just as it begins to smoke, remove it from pan. This should all take less then a minute! This toasting can be done on a dry pan or with a very, very small amount of oil. The chiles can be deveined and seeded before *or* after you do this.

Toasting Tips

• Larger dried chiles should always be toasted. Smaller dried chiles taste better when toasted, but it is not necessary.

•Cast iron fry pans are marvelous for toasting dried chiles

• Toasting in the broiler oven or on the barbecue is essentially the same as pan toasting. Little chiles are placed on a strip of aluminum foil or on a baking pan, and larger ones are toasted directly on the grill.

• Barbecue style woks are perfect for toasting smaller dried chiles outdoors. But watch them carefully and turn them frequently.

• Even outside, heed our warning about the capsaicin vapours.

After toasting

Once toasted, dried chiles are either *ground into a seasoning*, or are *rehydrated and mixed with other ingredients for sauces*. Although it is more convenient to toast many chiles at a time— there is a quality gained in toasting chiles *just before* grinding or rehydrating.

Grinding toasted chiles

When grinding chiles, it is most common to let them cool and then slit them open to remove the seeds. If the chiles are tiny (for instance chile de arbol, pequins, or piquins), the seeds are never removed. At this point, you simply *crush* them in the traditional mortar and pestle, or use a blender or food processor for larger volumes. Those tiny pequins can be crushed with your fingers— but for heaven's sake don't forget to wash your hands before you touch anything else!

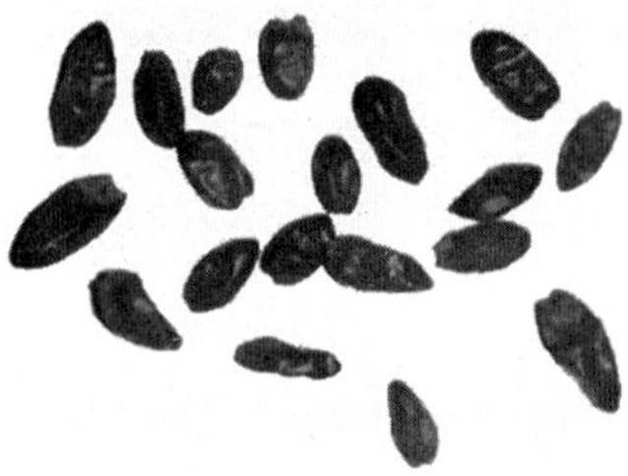

The Aztecs and other tribes actually used chile smoke as a weapon, like tear gas. Alas, that modern invention pepper spray uses this same principle.

Rehydrating Larger Dried Chiles

Place any toasted chiles in a bowl to cool before handling. Then, gently slice one side and remove all of the veins and seeds. The placental wall usually separates from the chile flesh, and these lighter colour 'strips' are easily removed. But make note, some recipes use the veins and seeds; in such cases, the seeds are removed and toasted independently and eventually added back to a purée. But most of the recipes we have listed in this book just tell you to dump those seeds and veins in the trash.

To rehydrate any toasted dried chile, pour very hot water over it and let it sit in a bowl. If chiles are large, very dry or thick skinned— use boiling water to begin. Let them sit in a water-bath until they soften. You may have to use a 'weight' to keep the chiles submerged during this soaking process. In Mexico, soaking doesn't take long because dried chiles are 'freshly dried'. However, chiles bought in the USA or Canada take a little longer to rehydrate.

It might take from 15 minutes to an hour depending on the chile. Allow sufficient soaking time in case it takes longer than a recipe suggests.

Using Rehydrated Chiles

Some rehydrated chiles are occasionally used whole. For example a rehydrated ancho chile can be used to make a special version of chile relleno. This dark 'stuffer dish' is delicious when crammed full of a mild white cheese. Or, dried anchos are sometimes cut into strips with a very sharp knife *before* toasting (to make a *dried raja*) and then soaked in a vinegar, sugar and water mixture to produce a delicious pickled condiment.

However, 'raw use' is unusual, and rehydrated chiles are most often used to make the purées that become the base for fantastic cooked sauces. After a dried chile has soaked, it is most often *'squished'* or blended into a pulpy liquid.

Purées

Rehydrated chiles can be crushed with a simple mortar and pestle— but a faster and convenient method is to liquefy the softened chiles in blenders (*licuadoras*) or food processors. In effect, the end result is a rich purée.

Place the soaked chiles in a blender and add a small amount of liquid in order to make a smoother purée— add more liquid if the chiles seemed to be *tough* after rehydrating. This

The names of chile dishes can get a little confusing when dried chiles are used. Mexican cooks do not use a single word to describe what we would call a '**sauce**'. We prefer to describe the rehydrating and grinding of softened chiles with the word *purée*. A special cooking sauce made with this purée is called an ***enchilada***— literally meaning *covered in* chile purée. In Mexico, they complicate things even more by using names of the chile used in the cooking sauce; for instance *enchocolada* refers to dish baked with a dark brown poblano. A purée can have ingredients added to it, and be used as a condiment. In this case, it is simply a **salsa**.

additional liquid can be a few tablespoons of the same water used to soak the chiles, But some recipes suggest that you discard the original soaking water and replace it with another liquid— fresh water or a vinegar-water mixture, or a hearty broth. Some creative purées use fruit juice.

The resulting purée can then be used to make a *cooked salsa* that is used as a *baking sauce* for vegetables, seafood, chicken, turkey or other meat dishes. Because these sauces are always part of some other dish, we have learned to cook meat ahead of time and reserve some of the broth as the added liquid when we rehydrate dried chiles.

We will tell you more about the process of rehydrating and cooking dried chiles for sauces in our recipes for the smoothies.

Poaching Dried Chiles in Oil

There are some recipes that work better if dried chiles have been *softened in a very hot oil* before they are soaked in water. Some complex moles and even some enchilada sauces suggest that you use this approach everytime. We encourage you to try this technique for softening dried chiles— but do not overcook chiles in the hot oil because you will make them bitter.

When you soften with oil, it is always best to remove the seeds and veins *before* you heat the chiles. So, make a slit in a dried chile and remove the stem, the veins and the seeds and discard them.

Then, place about 3 to 6 tbsp. of cooking oil in a frying pan (cast iron again) and heat at a moderately high temperature. Do not let the oil smoke, but try to get it as hot as possible. Now, drop the dried chile pieces into the hot oil and *count slowly to two* before turning them over and count to two once again. Remove them immediately! Drop the poached chiles into boiling hot water and let them soak until softened.

Once the chiles have softened in the water, drop them into a blender or a food processor and add a small amount of fresh water. Do *not use* the water in which you soaked the chiles, and *do not add too much* water. As general rule of thumb, add about 1/3 of a cup of liquid for every 6 whole larger chiles that are rehydrated.

Skin Tips

As you already know from reading about fresh chiles, roasting chars the outer skin and makes it easy to remove. But a toasting or oil poaching process doesn't produce exactly the same effect on dried chiles. The outer skin cannot be easily peeled from dried chiles. So, with dried chiles, do one of 3 things with the outer skin:

- ***just leave the skin on*** and liquefy it along with every thing else in the blender.
- liquefy the rehydrated chile in processor, and then remove the pulp and ***strain it through a cheesecloth or a fine colander*** to remove the outer skin bits.
- or, as Diana Kennedy suggests, ***butterfly*** the rehydrated chiles to expose the inner pulp, and then ***scrape this 'fleshy part' off with a sharp knife***. Place only the smooth pulp in the blender for further processing.

We most often use the first method as it retains a "smoky" flavour in a toasted chile— and frankly ***it's the easiest***. But, if you want to produce an extra special smooth paste, then you use either the second or third technique.

Using the purée

So, you have now turned a whole dried chile into a liquid pulp or purée. In the next section we tell you what you can do with this stuff to make either salsas or sauces . Sometimes, we liquefy a bunch of dried chiles ahead of time and produce the wonderful pulpy paste. We put this purée in a jar, close it tight and leave it in the back of the fridge for a few days or even weeks. There is some deterioration of flavour over time, but its offset by the convenience of having it at hand.

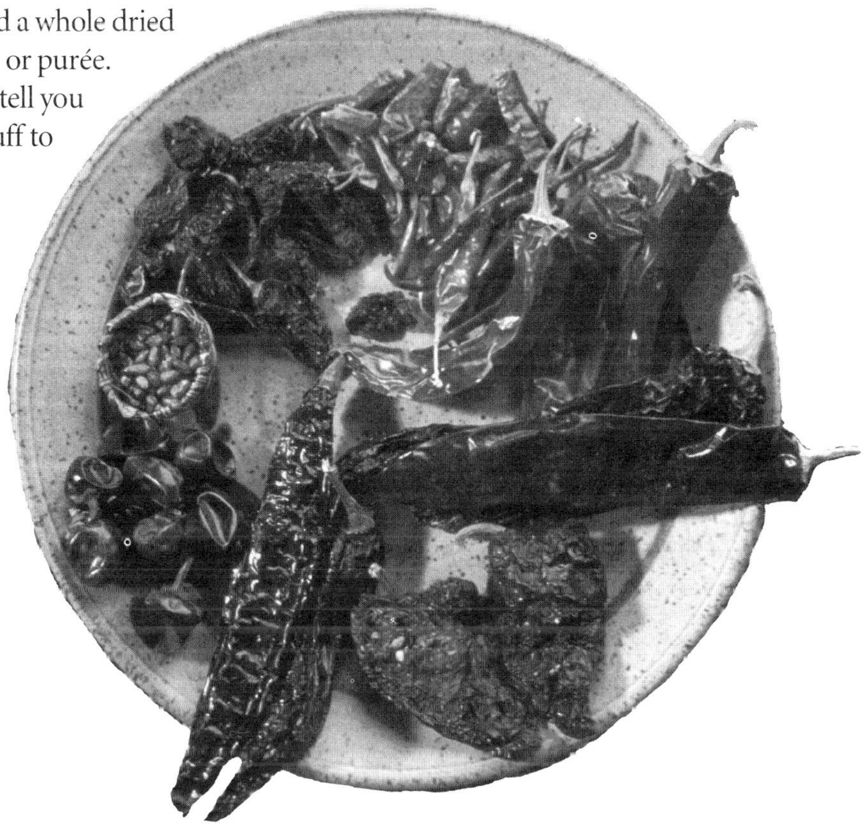

REHYDRATING TIPS

• To speed up the softening process we occasionally use a microwave (*zap for just a few seconds*) to periodically warm up the chile and bath solution. It's easy to overcook a dried chile in a powerful microwave, so do this with caution.

• If a chile appears extra tough or brittle, the oil method of toasting usually works better. See page 100.

• Chiles can acquire a bitter taste if they are overcooked or if you let them sit too long in the water. Do not let them sit more than 1 hour before you remove them from the water.

• If the dried chile is very fresh and pliable use the same soaking liquid to make the purée. If they're harder and older, it's best to use fresh water.

• The amount of liquid to add varies, but use about 1/3 of a cup for every 6 whole rehydrated chiles.

UTENSILS AND CLEAN-UP

• Use a wooden spoon or stainless steel spoon when working with rehydrated chiles. Plastic spatulas stain.

• If you spill rehydrated chiles or paste on a counter, wipe a bit of vegetable oil on it to help clean it up.

TIPS FOR POACHING IN OIL

• Keep a sauce pan of boiling water beside the frypan. Move the chiles from the hot oil directly into this water.

USING BLENDER/FOOD PROCESSOR

• Blenders and processors require different skills. We most often use a food processor, but in Mexico they most commonly use a blender.

• Whatever your choice, you should be careful to go slowly and not overprocess.

• Use a 'pulse' setting whenever possible.

Smoothies

They're the smoothies! So called because they're primarily used to make those rich-oh so smooth- salsas that are the soul of Mexican cuisine.There are many, many varieties of dried chiles but once again in this book we'll be exploring two of the most widely available- the saucy reds and the exotic ancho.

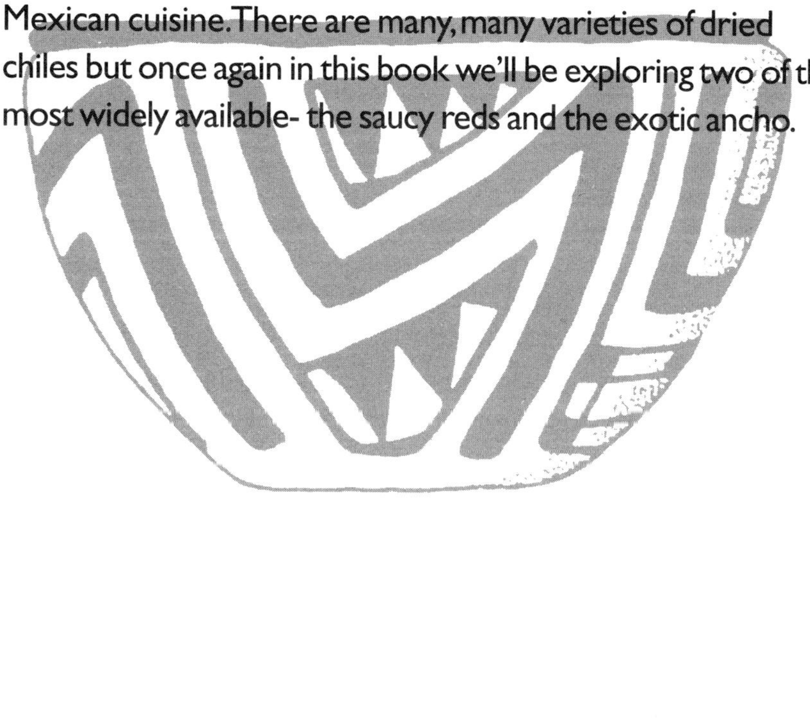

The Mercado La Merced is a giant market in downtown Mexico City

Larger Dried Chiles

These chiles are called everything from *reds* or *colorados*, *red California chiles*, *red New Mexico chiles* or sometimes they're just called a *ristra* chile. These chiles are a brighter red and have a shinier and smoother skin than ancho chiles (dried poblanos) .

There are major differences among the varieties in terms of heat and flavour, but the cooking and the preparations are all the same. Of course, if you're worried about too much heat you'll want to know whether a dried red chile is *picante* or *mild*. When you buy a New Mexico State chile ristra you're probably getting a *sandia* chile that is thin-skinned and is one of the hotter of the USA reds. In Mexico, the *guajillo* or the smaller *puya* chiles are comparable in picante quality.

The dried reds grown in Arizona are a bit milder. These are used by the Santa Cruz Chili and Spice Company in Tumacacori, Arizona to make a fresh chile paste that is used widely for *enchiladas* in Southern Arizona. The England family waits until the chiles turn red on the bush, and then they immediately process them and their natural juices into a paste. This canned chile purée removes several steps from the preparation and rehydration process, and we think it is a wonderful product. It has a unique flavour— a little sweeter and milder than most other dried long red chiles. Unfortunately, it is hard to find outside of southern Arizona.

Visit Santa Cruz Chile Company's charming retail outlet near the Tumacacori Mission and National Monument on the Nogales highway. Their canned chile paste is distributed throughout the southwest. Buy a small jar or large can when travelling in Arizona.

It can be ordered on the internet through http://www.sunlandimports.com/santa.htm

The reds or colorados are used to make enchilada *sauces* (which literally means *chilied*)— or they are added to other dishes like Tex-Mex chilis, Mexican stews (*guisos, guisados)* or regional favourites like *chilaquiles*. All red chile sauces have a complex flavour that reflects the soil and climate where peppers were grown. A red sauce flavour is not as rich or as full as an ancho sauce (described in the next section). Rather, this type is sharper and perhaps a bit more pleasantly bitter. Picante levels range from mild to medium hot.

A Basic Red Chile Sauce

Finally, we can tell you what to do with the purée we described on page 99. It's used to *make a cooking sauce*— most commonly known as enchilada sauce.

The red sauce made from chile purée is central to many delicious regional recipes from the borderlands of Northern Mexico, California, Arizona, New Mexico and Texas. The sauce is prepared in an uncomplicated way— but chefs have little tricks to make their recipe unique. Some use elaborate formulas to mix and match dried chiles in search of a specific taste. Some add flour or other spices. You can experiment and add a few secret ingredients of your own— but for now let's focus on a basic version of the standard red sauce.

The name 'Tumacacori' means 'place where the round red peppers are found in abundance' in the language of the Tohono O'odham. It is a beautiful area just south of Tucson Arizona. The Santa Cruz Chile outlet is nearby.

Smoothie Recipes for Red Chiles

BASIC RED CHILE SAUCE

10 whole dried New Mexico chiles (or other American or Mexican dried red chiles)

1 tbs. high quality cooking oil

1 cup (5oz/150 grams) of finely chopped onions

2 garlic cloves, minced or pressed

1—2 cups of quality chicken stock

2 tbsp. of canola oil, lard or Crisco *(choose your fat!)*

salt to taste

Toast the chiles using the techniques described above (page 97). In the basic red sauce, it is best to *not* blacken chiles during roasting. Slit and discard the membrane and seeds after toasting and cooling. Bring water to boil in a sauce pan, and remove it from the heat. Add the deveined and deseeded chiles, and keep them covered by the hot water until they are soft (up to 1/2 hour). You may have to use a weight to keep the chiles submerged.

Meanwhile, heat the cooking oil in a heavy pan and sautée the onions until they are golden brown. Place the rehydrated chile pieces (see the note about skin on page **101**), onion, garlic and 1/2 cup of chicken stock in a food processor. Purée until very smooth! Use a sieve, and strain the smoothened purée back into another bowl to make a smoother sauce. Heat the remaining fat at medium heat (*lard is a delicious but forbidden luxury for most of us*) in the frying pan, and add the strained mixture back into the pan.

Stir constantly to mix the oil and chile purée, and cook for about 5 minutes. Finally, add additional chicken stock and cook on medium-low heat until it has the consistency of a medium-thin gravy. Add salt to taste. Remove from heat and use immediately, or store in the refrigerator for 3–5 days in a covered jar.

Optional: Pure chile powders can be used instead of the whole dried chiles. In this case, use 3/4 of a cup of dried chile powder. Increase the liquid to about 2—3 cups total. Use pure chicken stock, or thin the stock with an equal amount of water. Mix 1 cup of the liquid with the powder and cook it with onions and garlic in a sauce pan as described above. Gradually, add reserved liquid to the sauce in the pan and mix. Continue cooking until it thickens and has the consistency of light gravy. If necessary, thin with more liquid

In our opinion, a basic red sauce does not freeze well. It becomes too 'mealy' for our taste after thawing. But, we have prepared batches of this sauce and put them in canning jars when the sauce is freshly cooked. We've sealed these jars in a water bath using the rules we described earlier for canning. However, we only store these prepared enchilada sauces in the refrigerator for a few weeks before we use them up. This process is not recommended for long term storage or shelf storage because the acidic level is too low for canning.

In Mexico the most common red dried chile is the *guajillo.*

A shorter version of this is the *puya.* Specialty food stores often sell guajillos instead of New Mexico reds .

We find that these can be hotter than most New Mexico red chiles. However, they also have a wonderful smoky quality.

There are many variations for basic red sauce

- Diana Kennedy suggests that a super smooth sauce can be made by butterflying the chiles and using a paring knife to scrape the softened flesh off of the outer skin. Only the pulpy scraped flesh is added to the processor.
- Use a *mixture* of dried chile types instead of only New Mexico reds.
- Leave the seeds and membrane in the chile while it is puréed. The seeds can be strained out with a sieve or cheesecloth before cooking.
- Remove the seeds and *blacken them* in a pan. Blackened seeds can be crushed in a mortar and added back to the chile paste before cooking. This adds more heat, and changes the flavour a great deal. It is the special trick to successfully cooking several classic Mexican recipes.
- Add a little flour to the oil and brown it before adding the puréed chile paste into the sauce pan. This is a process akin to making a *roux* and it produces a thicker enchilada sauce with a darker colour and nuttier flavour.
- Use larger packages of crushed and pulverized *pure* red chile powder to make this salsa. Use about 3/4 cup of this paste instead of the dried chiles. You generally need to triple the liquids called for in a recipe when you use a powder. Be careful– many chile powders actually have other ingredients.
- If you are lucky, purchase bottles or cans of Santa Cruz Red Chili Paste. You substitute about 3/4 cup of this paste for the dried red chiles. This makes a wonderful sweet red chile paste.

Long green chiles are very versatile. Fresh green chiles are roasted, canned and sold whole. When they turn red, they are processed into a paste. Or they are allowed to dry and are later crushed into a pure chile powder. There are also prepared enchilada mixes.

Once you have prepared your supply of this wonderful red chile paste, you can make many of the classic Mexican dishes. Use it to make either of the following two variations of a classic Mexican dish called the *enchilada*.

CHEESE ENCHILADA

The Molinas are an extended family in southern Arizona, and two or three generations of brothers and sisters, aunts and uncles and cousins have operated some marvelous eating places over the years. One of the simplest and most delicious meals offered at Midway Molina is a simple cheese enchilada which is accompanied by a side order of refried beans (and cold beer of course). We'll never match their version of this classic, but this recipe meets our basic needs at home.

12 fresh corn tortillas (4"–5" across)

3/4 lb. (400 grm) of soft cheddar, colby, farmer, or mozzarella cheese or a mixture of all of these cut lengthways into 1/2" by 1/2" slices

1/4 cup cooking oil

1 1/2 cup of basic red chile sauce in a mixing bowl

1/4 cup finely chopped onion

1 cup of finely shredded lettuce

1/4 cup cilantro leaves *(optional)*

Place about 1/8" layer of oil in a frying pan and gently warm it. At the same time, prepare a 12"x10" casserole dish by lightly coating the inside surface with oil (spray oil is perfect), and pouring a thin level of chile sauce on the bottom. Using kitchen tongs, quickly pass a single tortilla through the warm oil to coat on both sides and then immediately drag it through a bath of the chile sauce. Lay this coated tortilla in the casserole dish, and place at least 2 cheese strips in the middle of the tortilla. Sprinkle about 1 tsp. of chopped onion on top of the cheese, and then roll the tortilla into a 'tube'. This is done by gently turning one side of the tortilla over the cheese, and then repeating from the other side of the tortilla. Position the rolled tortilla loosely against the end of the casserole dish. Repeat with the other tortillas until the casserole dish is filled with the rolled tortillas placed loosely side by side.

Pour the remaining sauce over top of the tortillas. If you like, crumble remaining cheese (or grate a little more) on top of the sauce.

Place in a preheated oven (375°F) and cook for about 20–25 minutes. Remove and let the dish sit a few minutes, and then serve 2 tortillas on a plate. Sprinkle with the chopped lettuce and cilantro. Serves 4 people.

In the American southwest, they are served with refried beans. Any side dish of beans goes well.

CHICKEN ENCHILADA

Our first experience with Mexican food was in Tucson Arizona where cheese (mostly longhorn) is used quite liberally. Many years later, after learning about other regional specialties, we discovered that cheese does not always have to be the central ingredient. For example, in central and southern Mexico, cheese is used sparingly and is usually a crumbly variety called queso fresco. This next dish can be adapted to your taste— top it with lots of grated longhorn, Monterey jack, or colby, or sprinkle it lightly with a crumbly white cheese. You can make a nice queso fresco topping by mixing crumbled feta cheese with parmesan (about 2/3 feta to 1/3 parmesan).

12 fresh corn tortillas (4"—5" across)

1 lb. (450 grams) of white boiled chicken breasts, cooled and shredded

1 tsp. crushed cumin seeds (*option: toasted*)

1/4 cup cooking oil

1 1/2 cup of basic red chile sauce in a mixing bowl

1/4 cup finely chopped onion

1 cup of finely shredded lettuce

1/4 cup cilantro leaves (*optional*)

1/2–1/4 cup grated cheese (your choice of longhorn, monterry jack, colby, feta, or parmesan)

Sprinkle the crushed cumin seeds over the cooked and shredded chicken.

Place about 1/8" layer of oil in a frying pan and gently warm it. At the same time, prepare a 12"x10" casserole dish by lightly coating the inside surface with oil (spray oil is perfect), and pouring a thin level of chile sauce on the bottom.

Using kitchen tongs, quickly pass a single tortilla through the warm oil to coat on both sides and then immediately drag it through a bath of the chile sauce. Lay this coated tortilla in the casserole dish, and place about 2 tbsp. of the chicken strips across the tortilla. Sprinkle about 1 tsp. of chopped onion on top of the chicken, and then roll the tortilla into a 'tube'. This can be done by gently turning one side of the tortilla over the cheese, and then putting the other side on top of this. Position the rolled tortilla loosely against the end of the casserole dish. Repeat with the other tortillas until the casserole dish is filled with the rolled tortillas laying loosely side by side.

Pour the remaining sauce over top of the tortillas. If you like, you can crumble some cheese on top of the sauce.

Place in a preheated oven (375ºF) and cook for about 20–25 minutes. Remove and let the dish sit a few minutes, and then place 2 or 3 tortillas on a plate. Sprinkle with the chopped lettuce and cilantro.

This goes extremely well with refried beans or any Mexican style beans.

Cook the chicken before you make your basic red paste. Reserve the chicken and use the broth as the liquid in your basic red sauce.

Variations in Preparation

• The tortillas are dredged through the oil to make them a little more flexible. If you have really fresh tortillas, avoid this step to reduce fat content.

• Some cooks reverse the order and drag the tortilla through the chile paste before they drag it through the oil. This produces a delicious enchilada—but there is more splattering and a messy kitchen.

• You can bypass both the oil dip and the sauce dip, but the enchiladas will probably be drier.

• Use flour tortillas instead of corn.

RED CHILAQUILES

We told you about a green chilaquile dish on page 51. There are many versions of chilaquiles from around Mexico and the biggest difference is the salsa in which the stale tortillas are cooked. During our time in Mexico City, we loved to try different 'State' versions of chilaquiles just to see how much difference the regional salsas made . Toks restaurant chain specialized in these regional breakfast dishes from around the Mexican Republic. There are great variations and every one is delicious. If you want to know more, turn to the end of the book where we provide a little description of some of sauces and how they are used in different dishes (page 183).

This next dish is a rather uncomplicated variation of a chilaquile using the basic red sauce described at the beginning of this chapter.

Oil for cooking

8 dry corn tortillas, broken into large pieces and fried in oil until golden brown (*but not necessarily crisp*)

1 cup of basic red chile sauce (p.106)

1 cup water

1 cup chicken broth

1/2 cup of the shredded chicken used to make the broth (*optional*)

crumbly white cheese (e.g. farmers, feta)

half container of plain low—fat yogurt (*optional*)

fresh cilantro to taste (*optional*)

Make the red sauce described above on page 106. Heat the oil in a fry pan and lightly fry the stale tortillas until they are golden. Set them aside for a minute on a paper towel. Add a little more oil to coat the fry pan and then add the red salsa mixture to the hot oil. Stir a little, and immediately add the chicken consommé and the water until you have produced a thick but runny liquid. Add the fried tortilla pieces into this mixture and stir it up. Pour everything into casserole dish, and top with the crumbly white cheese as a topping. The pieces of chicken can also be added for extra flavour. Add them after you add the broth to the frying pan.

Some people also spread fresh cream over the top— but we suggest you try a little fresh yogurt after the dish has been assembled.

Top with a little bit of cilantro.

Anchos

Among the many *dried* chiles, the ancho is the most popular in Mexico. Ancho, is the Spanish word for 'broad', and this term accurately describes this chile's shape. Anchos are flat, broad at the top and almost triangular in overall appearance. The ancho, the dried version of a fresh poblano, has a meaty, wrinkled flesh that is green or reddish brown in colour and darkens with age. A reddish-translucent tint when held up to light distinguishes high quality anchos from other dried chiles (*mulato, pasilla*). The ancho rates about a medium on the heat scale.

Anchos and their fresh version— the poblano.

Don't forget if a poblano comes from California, it's commonly called a *pasilla* whether it's fresh or dried

A true pasilla is quite different. It's long and black and is a dry chile. It's fresh form is the *chilaca*— common in Chihuahua.

The pasilla blends beautifully with other dried chiles, like anchos or reds, to make a rich, complex salsa and intense seasoners.

Believe it or not, there's a sophisticated 'grading' system for dried anchos (and there is probably a 'futures' market on quality anchos.) The highest rating goes to ancho chiles that have a *luminescent golden hue* when held up to light. The lower rated chiles are darker and also smaller. The best anchos are also soft and pliable, which indicates that they were recently dried. They're somewhat like raisins in this regard. Fresh raisins are soft and moist, but older ones are harder and not as pleasant to use. A fine quality ancho is a bit like a lighter coloured sultana raisin.

Anchos are undoubtedly the most versatile of dried chiles. They have a unique 'raisin like' flavour, and are also complex, rich and sweet. Anchos are used as shells for stuffing, as raja strips for flavouring— but are most often used to produce a base for very smooth salsas.

We appreciate finding any anchos in our neck of the woods, even the lower grade anchos sold by supermarket chains. Specialty Latino stores are most likely to stock superior grades if the owners can find them during buying trips. Snap up any ancho that lets light pass through in a golden translucent state. You won't regret it even if costs you a bit more— and you'll definitely appreciate the end result.

Smoothie Recipes for Anchos

This first sauce is very similar to the Basic Red Chile sauce that we described in the last section. In Mexico, the ancho is the preferred chile for making a basic working sauce. When it is made with the highest quality chiles— the kind that you can almost see through— it is indescribably light and delicious.

BASIC ANCHO SAUCE

8 ancho chiles

3 1/2 cups warm water

1 medium onion, chopped

2 cloves garlic, chopped

1/4 cup vegetable oil

1 can (8 oz) tomato sauce

1 tbsp. dried oregano leaves

1 tbsp. cumin seed

dash of salt

Toast the chiles and remove the stems, the seeds and the membrane. Cover them with warm water. Let them stand until softened (up to 30 min). Drain. Strain the liquid and reserve it. Cook the onion and garlic in the vegetable oil in a 2 quart saucepan until soft and tender. Stir in the softened chiles, 2 cups of the reserved liquid and all other remaining ingredients. Heat to boiling, and then reduce the heat. Simmer uncovered 20 minutes and let everything cool. Process everything in blender or food processor until it is very smooth. This is a great salsa to top stuffed chiles, and it makes a great enchilada sauce in place of the basic red sauce.

ANCHO PASTE

ancho chiles

hot water

Preheat oven to 350°F. Roast the chiles on baking sheet or cast-iron fry pan until they puff up and smell toasty. Remove the stem and the seeds. Place chiles in a small bowl and cover with hot water, allowing them to soak for 15–20 minutes. Place the chiles in a blender or food processor; add a small amount of the soaking liquid and process to a smooth puree, adding more liquid if needed. Will keep in refrigerator for several weeks. Add to soup, stews, or any liquid used to cook meats.

NOTE: it requires about 1/3 cup of water for every 6 softened anchos .

Variations for Basic Ancho Sauce

• One variation is to mix different chiles with anchos. A favorite is the mexican *pasilla*, which is a wonderful black colour and is very long. It makes the sauce darker, and adds a delicious pungent flavour.

• Purée the ancho separately and then add it back into the other ingredients as they are cooking. After everything is processed a second time the sauce is very, very smooth.

• Heat the ancho momentarily in hot oil before dropping into the water to rehydrate. This might be necessary for more inferior quality, more brittle or older anchos.

Anchos come in different colours, sizes and qualities, but they have a broad flat shape with a wrinkled surface. A longer pasilla chile is pictured beside two anchos.

ANCHO SAUCE WITH ORANGE JUICE

The next little salsa is a good example of the versatility of the ancho. Instead of using water, it uses orange juice. If you are adventurous, try mixing other fruit juices with the ancho.

1/4 cup of fine olive oil

6 high quality ancho chiles— deseeded and deveined

3 cloves of garlic

3/4 cup orange juice

salt to taste

Heat the oil in a heavy skillet or sauce pan. Add the anchos and fry until coated with the oil. Place the chiles, the remaining oil, and all of the other ingredients in a food processor or blender. Pulse and process until smooth. If the sauce appears to thick, add a bit more orange juice. Excellent on fish dishes and pork.

CARMEN'S SALSA

Without a doubt, this has become our favorite ancho salsa. It seems to perfectly complement the subtle taste of salmon. The recipe is based on one described in Reed Hearon's classic little book called Salsa. He gives credit to a friend of his from the Coyoacan neighborhood of Mexico City— "Carmen"— who scrambles egg and nopales with this salsa. We would really like to meet Carmen— because she created a masterpiece with just a few simple ingredients. We've used this salsa in many ways not described by Hearon. Try barbecuing a whole salmon (or salmon steaks) and covering the fish with this salsa about 5 minutes before it is done! The sugar content means that it can blacken on the barbecue— so wait until near the end of cooking to add this salsa.

3 ancho chiles (highest quality)

2 tbsp. apple cider vinegar

1 small cone piloncillo (Mexican raw sugar) or 3 tbsp. dark brown sugar

1 cup water

1/2 medium sized white onion, sliced and pan roasted until brown

3 cloves garlic, pan roasted until brown and soft and peeled

dash of salt

In heavy skillet, toast the chiles until they are brown and fragrant. Cool slightly and slit them open, and remove the veins and seeds. In a small saucepan, boil the vinegar the piloncillo and water. Add the chiles and simmer until the sugar has completely dissolved and chiles have softened. With fresh anchos, this only takes about 5 minutes, but with lesser quality anchos you might have to let the anchos sit in the liquid longer. Turn off the heat, and let the chiles soak in the liquid until they are soft. Let everything cool down, and then combine with all of remaining ingredients in a blender and purée until smooth. Make extra, and keep this in the refrigerator in a tightly closed jar.

SMOKY CHILE PESTO

This recipe is similar to the previous salsa, but oil is added to it. It has a slightly heavier consistency than Carmen's salsa.

3 ancho chiles, toasted, soaked and pureed
2 cloves garlic, minced
1/2 cup minced onion
1 tbsp. fresh cilantro, minced
1 tsp. fresh mint, minced
3 tbsp. safflower oil
4 tbsp. vinegar or lime juice
dash salt and pepper

Mix together garlic, onion, chiles, cilantro, mint and oil. Use it without the vinegar to brush on tender cuts of meat, chicken or fish after you have seasoned them with salt and pepper.

Add vinegar to this and use it as a marinade for meats.

Add chicken stock and use for basting meats which bake for longer time periods.

If you like pasta coated with a rich tomato sauce made from sun-dried tomatoes— then you try this pesto in place of the tomato sauce. Top with grated parmesan cheese.

CREAMY ANCHO SALSA

8 ancho chiles
1 small onion
4 small cloves garlic
1/2 cup olive oil
1/2 cup red wine vinegar
1/4 cup crumbled cream cheese
salt to taste

Toast chiles lightly. Remove veins and seeds. Cut chiles into small pieces and chop the onion and garlic. Mix with oil, vinegar and salt. Let sauce season for 2 hours. Serve, topped with crumbled cheese. Use with meats.

Pilon is a brown cane sugar. It is also called piloncilo, and panela. It comes in different sizes. Substitute brown sugar if you can't find this.

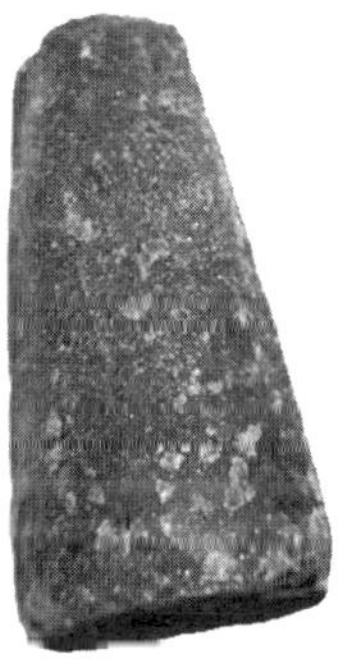

In Guanajuato, Mexico we came across a delicious local specialty using an ancho sauce. Called enchiladas mineras (or miners' enchiladas), these are tortillas topped with an ancho sauce, ancho strips, and potatoes. Finally, everything is covered with a roasted 1/4 chicken and an assortment of roasted vegetables.

DARK RED CHILE SAUCE

Here's something a little different— ancho chiles are combined with canned tomatoes. This can be served with enchiladas, rice, tacos etc. Or try a little bit of it tossed on a squiggly pasta like penne, or rotini.

4 ancho chiles—toasted, veins and seeds removed
1 cup canned tomatoes with juice
1 cup chopped onion
1 clove garlic
1 tsp. oregano
1/4 tsp. cumin
1/4 cup olive oil
1 tbsp. vinegar
tabasco sauce

Put chiles, tomatoes, onion, garlic, oregano and cumin into an electric blender and puree. Heat oil in a skillet. Add pureed sauce and cook about 10 minutes. Stir in vinegar and tabasco.

ANCHO and TOMATILLO SALSA

Here's an easy to make ancho salsa that also uses one of our favorite vegetables, the tomatillo (see page 151). It dates back to pre-Hispanic times. For added authenticity, serve this dish in a decorative molcajete. We suggest that you line the volcanic stone with lettuce leaves to keep the gritty stone from getting into your salsa. Serve with quesadillas (see the glossary on page 128), seafood (especially salmon), and beans— anything, really.

10 large tomatillos, husked
6 medium cloves garlic, peeled
1/2 medium white onion, peeled
4 ancho chiles—toasted, seeded and deveined
2 tsp. honey (*optional*)

Place tomatillos, 6 garlic cloves, the onion and chiles in medium saucepan. Cover with water and simmer uncovered for about 20 minutes. Drain and reserve cooking liquid. Purée the mixture in a molcajete, food processor or blender. Add about 1 cup of reserved liquid and crush, purée or mix until smooth.

Add a tiny bit of honey if you find the taste too acidic. This is not authentic, but it might suit your palate.

molcajete: a volcanic bowl with mortar. You can buy one for decorative purposes, but we really don't recommend that you actually grind chiles in the ones you see in tourist areas. If you use it for a salsa, always line it with clear wrap or a whole lettuce leaf to protect the salsa from picking up the fine grains of volcanic stone.

MANGO—ANCHO SALSA

Now if you want to get a little more adventurous with anchos here's a salsa that uses mangos and tomatillos. Not a sauce, but the result's terrific.

- **4 ancho chiles—toasted, deveined and seeded**
- **3 ripe mangos**
- **6 cloves garlic, roasted**
- **7 tomatillos**
- **8 plum tomatoes**
- **1 large onion**
- **2 limes**
- **1 tbsp. vinegar**
- **1 bunch fresh cilantro**

Dice the mangoes, tomatillos, tomatoes and onion and mix in large bowl. Add 1 tbs. vinegar and juice of 2 limes. Purée cloves of garlic and add to mixture. Crumble ancho chiles and add to mixture. Add cilantro. Mix until well combined.

Put in refrigerator and let sit 1/2 hr. before serving.

NOTE: this is a rare case where a recipe calls for raw tomatillos. You can cook them and then add them to the mixture.

STUFFED CHILE ANCHOS

We know— we know, "anchos aren't in the 'stuffer' chapter". But to show how imaginative one can get with these chiles we present a recipe that uses anchos as a casing for cheese. When choosing anchos for stuffing try to get the high quality ones that are soft, pliable and rather large. If the chiles are too dark and 'brittle' (see page 111) don't try this recipe.

- **6 ancho chiles—toasted and deseeded**
- **1 tbsp. oil**
- **10 oz (315 g) tomatillos (about 6)**
- **1/2 large onion, cut into chunks**
- **2 large tomatoes, cut into chunks**
- **1 cup thick cream (or yogurt)**
- **1 1/2 cups grated white cheese (Monterey jack)**
- **1/2 cup all purpose flour**
- **3 eggs, separated**
- **oil for frying**

Toast lightly, and then soak the ancho chiles in warm water for about 5 minutes. Drain.

Remove husks from tomatillos and cook in oil for a few minutes. Add onion for 3 more minutes and then tomatoes and cook for a few minutes more. Add cream, cover and cook until sauce begins to boil. Remove from heat.

Stuff chiles with cheese. Spread flour on a plate. Beat egg whites until they form stiff peaks and then stir in the yolks. Heat oil in skillet and set beside the chiles and the egg mixture. Dip each chile in flour until it is coated and then dip it in the beaten egg mix. Add chiles, one or two at a time to the pan and fry on each side until lightly browned. When serving, heat the sauce, add chiles to it, cover and cook until the chiles are warm.

The Pasilla Chile

Originally, we were not going to include this beautiful dried chile in our book. However, it now is sold in many places outside of Mexico, and we suspect that it is on its way to becoming a very popular ingredient. We also decided that we should tell you about it because we do use it in our recipe for chorizo powder (page 124). Remember, some parts of California use the name *pasilla* to describe a chile that is known as poblano everywhere else. Make sure that your pasilla is long and skinny and not short and broad.

The true pasilla is a dried version of the fresh *chilaca* chile. It is almost exclusively used in a dried state in Mexico. It is important in many sauces, and is a central ingredient in many moles.

The pasilla is long, thin and shiny black. Sometimes the black colour has a tinge of dark green running through it. Pasillas are about as long as the average New Mexico chile (about 6–8 inches, or about 15 cm). They are treated in the same way as anchos or dried red chiles. That is, they are toasted, rehydrated, and used as a purée base for more complex dishes.

The pasilla is most often used to mix with other dried chiles in a smooth salsa. However, here's a table salsa from Mexico that uses the pasilla chile.

SALSA PASILLA

3 pasilla chiles

1/4 cup of warm water

2 tomatoes (plum)

3 serrano chiles sliced in rings

1/2 onion

1 clove of garlic, roasted

1 tsp. of vinegar

3 tbsp. cooking oil

salt to taste

Deseed and devein the pasilla chiles. Remove the stem. Toast the pasillas until warm, but don't overcook them. Place in the warm water and let them rehydrate for 10 or 15 minutes. Quarter the tomatoes, and add them to a processor along with the serranos, onion, garlic and vinegar. Add the softened pasilla chiles without the liquid. Process until relatively smooth.

Heat the oil in a sauce pan, and add the purée back into it. Cook for 5 minutes and remove the sauce. Serve at room temperature.

Seasoners

Most are small-but they pack a very large punch.The chiltepin, pequin, tepin and de arbol are valued for their picante quality and most often used as seasoners.They are crushed and added as a spice or served as a condiment.They can also be used whole in soups, stir fries, and stews to heat them up and add flavour.

Rock Corral Canyon in Southern Arizona contains a 4–square mile reserve called the Wild Chile Botanical Area. It is located in the Coronado National Forest to the west of the Tumacacori Mission on Interstate–19.

This area is the northernmost range of the wild chiltepin. The 3 to 4 foot tall plants are scattered around the botanical reserve and are usually underneath desert hackberries. Attempts at growing chiltepins commercially have been unsuccessful.

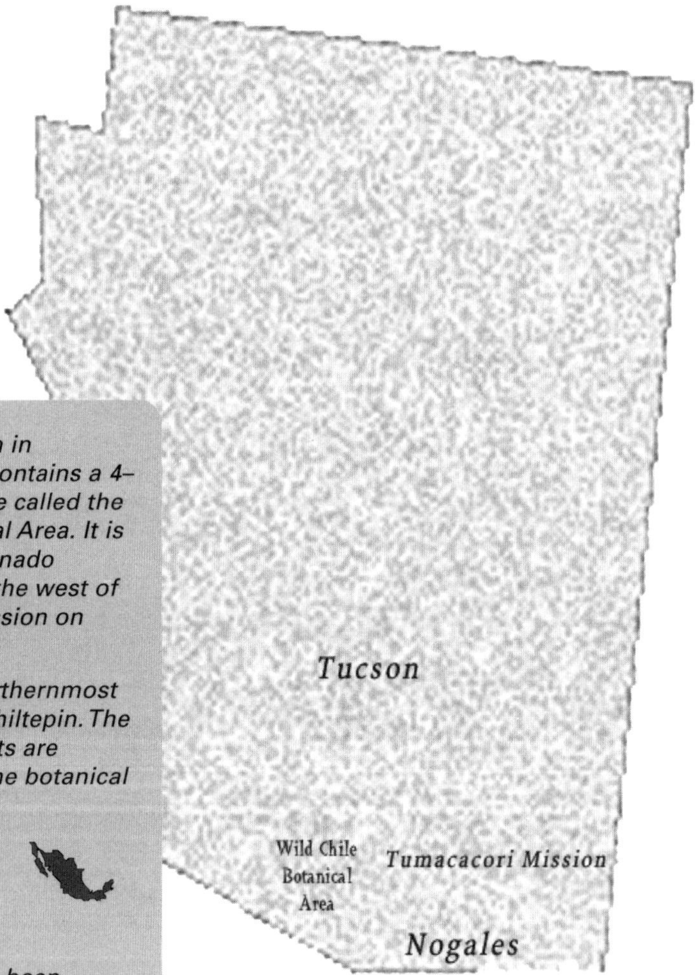

Chiles as Seasoners

The major purpose of seasoners is simple! They add a spicy quality to dishes just like the black pepper to which they were erroneously linked. Although larger dried chiles can be used as seasoners— it is more common to use the smallest varieties for this purpose. As we told you earlier, larger dried chiles are often toasted before they are used but the little guys are simply crushed and added to soups or other dishes. Sometimes they are also made into a paste which is used for marinades or as a liquid seasoner. There are some chile salsas made with these little chiles— and they make *very hot* table condiments.

Most of these chiles are purchased in *small pre-packaged* bags from grocery stores. Of course, in Mexico even the smallest chiles are available in bulk. Real chile aficionados keep a selection of small dried chiles on hand for personal use. The *chiltepin*, said to be the original ancestral chile, is the most sought after of this group. It still grows in remote areas of the Sonoran desert along the Arizona/Mexico border and can be difficult to find in markets. Expect to pay a lot if you do! Chiltepin cost upwards of $2.50 an ounce *more* than domesticated small chiles. *The popularity is attributable to the fact that these little guys are really rare and really hot*! One tiny chiltepin has the piquancy of five jalapeños and is said to be more potent than the legendary habanero.

An early Spanish explorer erroneously classified new world chiles as 'pepper' (pimientos) because the flavour reminded him of pepper from the old world (piper nigrum). As early as 1493, Peter Martyr used the term pepper in his chronicle of the Columbus expeditions in the Caribbean.

The first chile pepper seeds sent back by Columbus to Castille soon became a success in most of Europe, and from there they were introduced into the orient. The name 'chile pepper' stuck even though there is no botanical connection. This story is further complicated by the fact that there are at least 5 botanical species of chiles.

Chiltepin, pequin, tepin, and chile de arbol

Chiltepins and *piquins* are small, red and hot! A domesticated version of a wild round chiltepin is named the *pequin* or *piquin* (variations of the Spanish word for 'small'—*pequeño*). These two dried chiles are basically round in shape. There is an elongated version called a *tepin*. It too is very hot— rated as 8 on the heat scale. It's very small, less than 1/4 inch (.8 cm) long, and shaped like a tiny football. These cultivated varieties are widely available and are used commercially. For instance, *piquins* are commonly used to make hot bottled sauces.

The ancient character of small chiles is evident from archeological sites, and it is clear that small red chiles have long been integral to Southwestern Indian ceremonies. Many Native Americans consider chiles a gift from the gods to drive away evil and celebrate the harvest. A person who does not eat chiles can be suspected of being a sorcerer. A fascinating book on chiles and their cultural and symbolic importance in native life is Gary Nabhan's Gathering the Desert. For instance, he relates an intriguing creation story(*recorded in 1673*) from the Cora Indians of Mexico's west coast . This little fable talks about the *shocking effect* that chiles have— but it also tells us how much chile peppers are linked to culture and myth and celebration of harvest.

The maker created a man and a woman. The man was called Narama, the woman, Uxuu. He put them in a place with many fruits and minerals, but afterwards cast them out. Then, Narama began to sweat, and his sweat was changed into salt. The maker chose him to be the patron of salt, mescal and chile. As for Uxuu, He made her matron of all the seeds and fruits of the summer, and of watering the earth with rain. Other creatures peopling the earth were assigned to be the nurturers of additional foods, vegetable or animal.

A few days after having made these arrangements, the Maker invited all these people to a fantastic fiesta. He set a table in the middle of the earth, and each creature brought the foods entrusted to them, to share. Narama was among the last, and he came naked, covered with salt. After everyone was already seated, he presented himself at the table, took salt from his face and sprinkled it upon the foods. Then he reached down, and his testes turned into chile pods. He began to sprinkle their spice onto all of the foods.

This crude action annoyed all the other patrons, who angrily scolded Narama. To this, he replied that if the others could provide the fruits, fish, fowl, seeds and vegetables that were the basic staples of the fiesta, why could he not provide something that these foods needed to be truly tasteful? He declared that there was nothing so necessary as salt and chile. If they would just try the food both with and without these ingredients, they would know that in their hearts. They ate and not only became satisfied, but enthusiasts.

Quoted from Gary Nabhan, Gathering the Desert, pp. 123-4. University of Arizona Press.

Some of us will never encounter this mystical chile that the Cora saw as the beginning of the hot food adventure, but there are several options to the sacred chiltepin. The most common substitute is probably a larger *chile de arbol* (dried red tree chile).

The *chile de arbol* is often confused with a *dried version of the serrano*, but it's a distinct variety. *Arbol* is the Spanish word for 'tree' even though a chile de arbol grows on a short bush. Fresh versions of both the chile de arbol and the serrano ripen to a bright red as they are drying. Once fully dried, the colour gradually darkens. The chile de arbol is about 1–2 inches (2.5–5 cm) long, very hot, and is highly valued as a spice. Luckily, it's available at many markets.

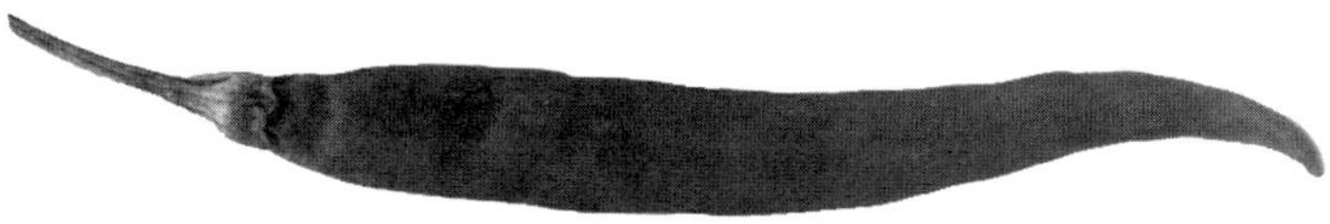

A similar chile, also readily available is the *chile de japon*. It is sometimes confused with the chile de arbol. The *japonesa* is a small cayenne variety (a different species) and, as you might guess, is widely grown in the orient. Like the chile de arbol, it's very hot and can be used as a substitute if the de arbol is unavailable. Since not much is done with these chiles other than crushing them or mixing seasoning pastes, you probably wouldn't notice a big difference in your recipes.

We've already told you how to grind these seasoners (pages 92-94) but here are a few recipes you might want to try. We'll present two short seasoner recipes using bigger dried chiles, but the majority of seasoners depend on the little hot chile peppers.

When rainy season (Aug.-Sept.) hits Sinaloa Mexico, the wild chile plants in the hills burst into fruit. Young boys hike into the hills, swim in the pools which appear, and also collect the fresh green version of chiltepin chiles. They package them in little plastic bags and sell them to tourists passing down the highway. Some boys tell stories about chile burns from stuffing too many fresh berries into their pockets, This fresh chile is an important ingredient in a shrimp dish called aguachile. The fresh chiles are not available in modern markets.

Seasoner Recipes

HOT SALSA DE CHILE DE ARBOL

3 whole tomatoes

1/2 small white onion, chunked

1/2 cup water

2 tbsp. vegetable oil

12 chiles de arbol

3 garlic cloves

2 tbsp. vinegar cider

salt to taste

Roast the tomatoes until blackened. Simmer the chiles, the onion and garlic in hot water in a small pan until they are all soft. Drain, reserving 1/4 cup of the cooking liquid. Transfer the mixture, the reserved liquid, tomatoes and the remaining ingredients to a blender. Purée until smooth. Chill for at least 1 hour.

This is very hot, but is a nice addition to soup. You can toast the chiles before soaking.

CHILE DE ARBOL SALSA VERSION 2

12 to 14 chiles de arbol

2 tbsp. cider vinegar

2 cloves garlic (roasted)

1/2 tsp. McCormick's oregano

1/4 tsp. toasted cumin seeds crushed

1/2 cup of water

salt to taste

Toast the chile pods in a hot frying pan until they are warmed and slightly blackened. Add the vinegar, the roasted garlic, the oregano, and the cumin seeds to a blender or a food processor. Add a small amount of the water (about 1-2 tbsp.) and pulse. Add a little bit more water and pulse again. Continue until all of the water is used up and the chile paste is relatively smooth.

This is very, very hot!

OAXACAN PEANUTS

Here's a wonderful quickie appetizer served regularly in Oaxaca (pronounced 'wa-hawk-ah') with cold beer, tequila and mescal. The garlic cloves can be left whole or chopped.

15 small dried red chiles, crushed

6 cloves garlic, chopped or left whole

2 tbs. olive oil

2 lbs. Virginia or Spanish peanuts

Combine all ingredients and spread on a baking pan. Bake for about 15 minutes in a 350°F oven. Remove from oven and let stand for awhile before serving. Ground cumin and salt can be added to taste.

RED CHILE OIL

Add crushed red chiles to olive oil and you have a whole new cooking ingredient. Herbs like rosemary, thyme or bay leaves can be added too.

- 1/2 cup olive oil
- 1 1/2 tsp. red chiles, crushed
- 1 tsp. rosemary leaves, chopped

Combine all ingredients and let stand for a couple of days. Strain the oil removing chiles and herbs before using the oil.

TOMATO–CHILTEPIN SALSA

Here's a tomato based salsa that's brought to life with 1/2 cup of dried chiltepins. Piquins or chiles de arbol can be substituted.

- 8 ripe roma tomatoes
- 1 onion cut in large chunks
- 6 cloves garlic
- 1/2 cup dried chiltepins— toasted and crushed
- 1 cup water

Toast the tomatoes, onion and garlic. Purée in a blender with the chiles. Add water until you achieve the desired consistency.

THE CHILTEPIN CHALLENGE

We hesitate to even suggest the following recipe! Obviously it's only for those who see chiles as a challenge! Well, we double dare you to try this. It may be your Waterloo! Keep in mind that in every heat scale one tiny chiltepin is hotter than the habanero, and is equal to about 5 jalapeños. A tiny drop of this concoction will fire up any number of otherwise innocuous dishes.

- 1 cup dried chiltepins
- 6 cloves garlic, peeled
- 1 tsp. Mexican oregano
- 2 tsp. ground cumin
- 1/2 cup water
- 1/2 cup cider vinegar

Toast the garlic and the oregano. Purée in a blender with all other ingredients. Makes about 1 cup.

CHILE CHEESE

You can add almost anything to cream cheese, so why not crushed chiles.
Here's a combination that can be served as a dip or spread.

8 ounces cream cheese

1 tbsp. chiltepins, crushed (*substitute other dried chiles as necessary*)

2 tbsp. cilantro, chopped

1/4 cup red onion, chopped

Let cheese soften at room temperature, or add a bit of yogurt or sour cream to make it more manageable.
Stir in remaining ingredients. Refrigerate.

Tabasco, the famous Louisiana sauce has a direct connection to the Mexican State ofTabasco. An American Soldier who was part of the 1846 invasion of Mexico brought back chile seeds and gave them to his friend Andrew McIlhenny. This family company is very protective of its product and has launched several lawsuits against its competitors. Ironically, a large part of the chile crop must be grown in other countries because of problems with blight. The company also weathered a major lawsuit which claimed that the McIlhenny recipe was in the public domain before it was claimed as a family right.

CRISPY CHILE POTATOES

Crushed and dried red chiles can be sprinkled on just about any vegetable dish. They can also be stir–fried in oil and this oil can then be used for cooking. Here's a way to add crushed dried chile to potatoes. These are oven baked but you can also add a few sprinkles of dried chiles to mashed potatoes, scallops or sprinkle with sour cream on baked potatoes.

1/4 cup olive oil

2 tsp. dried oregano

6 medium sized potatoes

2 tsp. crushed dried red chiles

Peel and quarter potatoes. Heat the oil in a fry pan and sautée the oregano briefly. Add the potatoes and stir until completely coated. Place the potatoes on cookie pan and sprinkle them with dried chile. Roast in a 350ºF oven until cooked. The outside should be very crispy.

RICE RICO

And, if you prefer rice, try this simple spicy mixture.

1/2 cup onion, finely chopped

3 dried red chiles crushed

2 tbsp. of olive oil

2 cups boiling water

1 cup white rice

Sauté onion and chiles in oil. Add rice, and heat until rice turns opaque. Add water and bring to a boil. Lower the heat and cover. Simmer until the rice has absorbed all the liquid.

DE ARBOL–ANCHO

Here are a couple of salsas that use chiles de arbol.

1 ancho chile—cleaned and seeded

4 chiles de arbol—seeds removed

1 can tomatoes or 8 large ripe tomatoes

1 tbs. vinegar

Toast all of the chiles using the instructions found earlier on page 97. Place the ancho and chiles de arbol in a pot and cover with boiling water. Let stand until soft— about 15 minutes. Remove the chiles and place in blender or food processor. Add the can of tomatoes and the vinegar and blend until smooth.

If using fresh tomatoes roast before blending.

Makes about 2 cups.

DE ARBOL–TOMATILLO

18–25 tomatillos—husked and roasted until soft

6 cloves garlic—roasted

4–6 chiles de arbol

1/4 cup onion, chopped

Toast the chile de arbol using the instructions found on page 97. Roast the tomatillos using the instructions described on page 152. Place the tomatillos in blender along with the garlic, chiles de arbol and onion. Blend until smooth. Makes about 3 cups.

This sauce can be used as a condiment with quesadillas, tacos and chalupas but is particularly good with plain old pork.

When we're in Mexico, we try to avoid eating on the 'street'– even though the food is incredibly tempting. One thing that Jim can't seem to resist is a delicious soup called pozole, which consists of lime-soaked corn kernels and shredded meats. It is served in a bowl, and the patron liberally adds to the bowl from side dishes of crushed chile powder, chopped onions and radish slices.

Quesadilla: this is simply the Mexican equivalent of a cheese sandwich. Place soft melting cheese on a fresh corn or flour tortilla, lay on one sprig of cilantro. Fold the tortilla in half and heat until the cheese melts.This is suprisingly tasty and addictive.Try it with cottage cheese instead of a melting cheese. Of course it needs a fresh salsa to make it perfect.
Chalupa: a thick tortilla in the shape of a 'boat'. Fillings are put in the middle

Seasoning recipes based on larger dried chiles.

Most of the seasoners rely on the little dried red chiles, but there are a few cases where larger chiles are also important. For instance, chorizo powder is a combination of different dried chiles like the large thin *pasilla* and the short broad *ancho*. Also, many spice mixtures for the wonderful tamales of Mexican cooking are based on exotic combinations of large and small dried chiles. We'll give you an example of each of these uses before we move on.

There is not much to tell you about cooking techniques. Perhaps the only thing that you might want to know is that all of the ingredients in a seasoning mixture can be dried roasted on a comal or a cast iron fry pan. We never make these mixtures without toasting ingredients over a dry heat.

The dry ingredients can blacken very quickly, so they have to be carefully watched while heating. Allow everything to cool a little after toasting, and then add everything to a blender or a grinding mill.

Ingredients for a special tamale seasoner are roasted before grinding. Pasilla chiles, ancho chiles, cumin, bay leaf, oregano and garlic are roasted dry . These are put in a blender and mixed with annato paste.

HOMEMADE CHORIZO POWDER

Chorizo sausage is a favorite dish along the Mexico –American Frontier, and many people purchase freshly made sausage links that are richly seasoned with dried chile peppers and vinegar. It is possible to buy several brands of chorizo powder mixtures throughout the southwest United States. Using these mixes, a cook browns a favorite ground meat mixture and pours on the powder. One great mix comes from National Spices in Phoenix Arizona. But if you can't find a pre-mixed version you can blend your own using the following recipe.

1/4 cup ground pasilla chile, seeds removed

1/4 cup ground ancho chile,seeds removed

1/4 tsp. ground cloves

1/4 tsp. ground cinnamon

2 garlic cloves, minced

1 tsp. oregano

1/2 tsp. sugar

1 tsp. salt

1/2 cup hot water

1/4 red wine vinegar

Toast the dry ingredients , and mix all of the ingredients to form a thick smooth paste. For a hotter mixture, add 3 or 4 finely crushed chiles de arbol or 6–8 chile piquins. Add this mixture to any ground sausage to make a version of tasty chorizo. We used this chorizo with ground turkey to produce the tasty topping for Baby-T's on page 86.

JAIME'S SPECIAL SEASONING

Tamales are a wonderful Mexican staple that come in many variations. The tamale starts with a masa dough (the corn masa used for making tortillas) and adds oil and sometimes seasonings. The dough is processed until extremely light, and then flattened on a corn husk, banana leaf or even an avocado leaf. A cooked filling is placed in the middle of the dough, and then it is carefully rolled up for steaming. The end result is a special dumpling of incomparable quality. You'll have to learn about tamales elsewhere (see any of Diana Kennedy's books)— but we will tell you about making a special seasoning that can be used in making tamales.

This seasoning mix was a key part of Jim's "Best of Show" prize winning recipe in the Chile Pepper Magazine Cooking contest.

This mixture can be made in a batch and stored in tightly sealed jars for general use as a seasoner. It uses large dried chiles and small dried chiles. If you can't find all of the ingredients you can mix and match.

1-2 dried pasilla chiles– deveined, deseeded, toasted and crushed

1-2 dried ancho chiles– deveined, deseeded, toasted and crushed

1/4 tsp. toasted sesame seeds– crushed

1/2 tsp. toasted unshelled pumkin seeds– toasted and puffed

1/4 tsp. cumin seeds—toasted and crushed

2 garlic cloves– toasted and crushed

1 bay leaf– toasted

1/8 tsp. ground black pepper

1/2 tsp. ground annato powder

1/8 tsp. thyme powder

1/4 tsp. cayenne powder

2 tsp. pure red chile powder

Toast the dried pasilla and ancho chiles. Set aside to cool. Toast the sesame seeds until they have browned, and set them aside to cool. Toast the unshelled pumpkin seeds until they are very dark and have puffed. The pumpkin seeds will expand like popcorn, so use a cover for the pan for this. Set these aside to cool. Toast the cumin seeds (*comino*), garlic and bay leaf and set them aside to cool.

Break the chiles into small pieces and add them along with all of the other ingredients to your spice mill or processor. Grind until you have a relatively fine powder.

Put this spice powder in a sealed container and use as a seasoner for soups, meats, tamales or whatever inspires you.

Pumpkin seeds can be roasted.

Chipotles

The chipotle is hot! And we don't just mean spicy. This dried chile has a smoky exotic flavour that has recently become a 'hot ingredient' in upscale southwestern restaurants. It's mixed into everything from mustard to mayo. And once you savor its smokiness you'll know why. Who would ever guess that this exotic chile is simply the smoke dried version of the humble jalapeño?

The process of smoking chiles is very ancient, and the Aztecs did it on a regular basis.

Chipotle History

We've reserved a separate chapter for the *chipotle* (also spelled *chilpotle* or *chipocle*) because it's a very special chile used both for sauces and seasonings. Mexican peoples have been preserving thick-fleshed chiles with a smoking-process since at least Aztec times (12th&13th centuries), and the techniques have changed very little. The popularity of this process remains very high, and even today about 20% of Mexico's fresh jalapeño crop is smoked or specially dried to create this type of chile.

There are many varieties of chipotles available in Mexico. The *meco* is a big tan coloured smoked chile made by curing the ordinary jalapeño with a heat process. It is about 2"-3" (5-8 cm) long with a thick leather-like skin. The *morita* is more common in Canada and the USA, and it is smaller, rounder, redder and more wrinkled than the meco. It actually comes from a *mora* chile which looks like a small red jalapeño but is shaped more like a fresno chile.

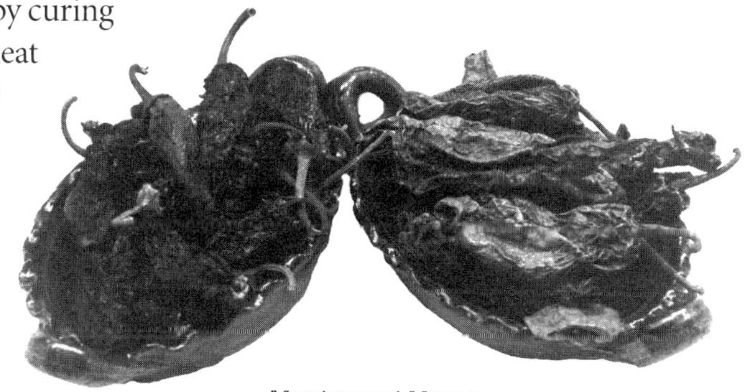

Moritas and Mecos

Flavour and heat levels in smoked chiles depend on many things— such as the origin of the fresh chile and the specific smoking technique used. The type of wood used also creates interesting variations in flavour. Smoking chiles is big commercial business in Mexico, and chipotles are available in bulk at all markets as *loose dried chiles* or *canned* in a special sauce (*en adobo*). Specialty markets in larger American and Canadian cities also carry supplies of loose fresh chipotles and the canned version. Some people are even fortunate enough to have access to freshly smoked chiles made by small-scale local producers in some parts of the United States. Jacqueline Higuera McMahan describes parts of California where home smoking of chiles is an elaborate ritual.

In the southwestern U.S., some people are now "smoking their own." If you're interested in finding out more about this intriguing and rather specialized activity we refer you to a book by Josephine Higuera McMahan called Chipotle Chile Cook Book. This book, one of many by the Calif. chef and writer, will tell you everything you ever wanted to know about this exotic chile.

Technically, commercial chipotles— the tan coloured mecos— are not smoked chiles. They're

preserved by forced-air drying.

Smoking chiles involves digging a smoke trench and linking it to a firepit. The chiles are placed at the trench end of the pit, and the smoke passes over them as it escapes into the atmosphere. Outside of Mexico, people have experimented with wet and dry smoking using special smoker units. Most of us must content ourselves with buying a few dried chipotles from small bottles or in small cellophane bags at specialty stores.

Why are they smoked?

Why aren't *jalapeños* or *mora* chiles air or sun dried like most other chiles? It's because they're too fleshy and air drying takes too long. It's also clear that the chiles acquire an intense smoky flavour that is addictive.

Most chipotles are jalapeños which are heat processed when they're green. They're about 3 inches (8 cm) long and a wood-tan colour. In some places, these longer types of smoked chile are very hard to find, and one is more likely to find the reddish and smaller *morita*.

It's easier to find *canned* chipotles and many people now prefer to buy chipotles in this form. Canned chipotles are also packed in a tasty *adobo* sauce which is a dark mixture of *ancho* chiles and tomatoes. These *chipotles en adobo* are puréed (sauce and all) to make a very spicy salsa, or the chiles are removed from the adobo and chopped for other uses..

Chipotles en adobo have a wonderfully different flavour than *rehydrated* loose chipotles. We've come to prefer the *chipotles en adobo* because they're easier to use and because the adobo sauce adds a terrific extra flavour. Check out Latin American or Mexican markets for canned chipotles en adobo. Some producers like Herdez make a very rich *ancho* adobo, whereas other companies use a simple tomato paste. Difficulties in cross-border labeling play havoc with supplies and create limitations on the range of specific brands available from Mexico.

In a pinch, buy a bottle of Herdez's Bufalo Chipotle Sauce and keep it on your shelf next to the H-P sauce. Pretty soon, the H-P sauce will be covered with dust.

We are definitely not telling you to forget about simple dried bulk chipotle (i.e. without the sauce). If you see them— *buy them and bring them home*. There is a great deal that you can do with them— including making your own special chipotle en adobo sauce.

Chipotles are hotter than the jalapeño because the smoking process concentrates the capsaicin in the dry flesh . It's simple to understand how this makes chiles hotter— water from the flesh evaporates but the capsaicin doesn't and it becomes more concentrated in the dried chile. But, most smoked chiles available to the average person have a very tough skin that requires *long soaking periods* to rehydrate. Because of this, we recommend that you soften the chipotle by heating it in hot oil before you drop it into the water to rehydrate. (See page 100). To make sure that the full impact of smoking remains with the chile, we also suggest that you use some of the soaking water when you make purées from this chile. Hopefully, you'll be able to find 'freshly smoked' chipotles for your cooking—but even if you don't the older ones will still produce a flavour that is absolutely unique.

The word chipotle is based on the Nahuatl words 'chil' for chile and 'poctli' for smoke and can actually refer generically to any smoked chile. But these days it is used almost exclusively in reference to the ripened and smoked jalapeño or mora. In Mexico, the varieties have very specific names like meco, morita or Vera Cruz.

Chipotles have an intoxicating effect and we are convinced that they also contain an addictive substance. Once you've tried the distinctively rich and complex flavour of this little gem you'll be hooked. You'll find yourself craving chipotles as stuffers, as salsas, as a barbecue sauce, or as seasoners for soups and stews. There is no substitute for this dried chile!

Chipotles keep for months in a closed jar or container or they can be frozen quite easily. If you open a small can of chipotles and only use a couple, the other chiles will keep in the refrigerator for several days or you can put them in small containers and keep them in the freezer for longer periods.

The jalapeño is one of the most versatile chile peppers. It is available fresh, pickled, smoked, canned in a sauce, and in bottled liquid form.

Herdez produces an excellent brand of chipotle en adobo. Their adobo sauce uses ancho chiles. The company sponsors research on Mexican Cuisine in the cultural context and have funded several quality magazines about the history of food in Mexico.

Here are some simple, popular chipotle recipes to try. We include a basic chile en adobo, and albondigas (meatballs) in chipotle— a popular dish in Mexico City.

Chipotle Recipes

HOMEMADE CHIPOTLE EN ADOBO

With this recipe, you can make your own home version of chipotle en adobo. We think that it tastes better than almost any commercial brand with the possible exception of the Herdez product. Make a batch of this and save it for your use in other chipotle recipes.

1/4 lb. chipotles (about 25)
2–3 anchos
2 qt. boiling water
2 large tomatoes, roasted
1 tbsp. olive oil
1 head garlic
2 bay leaves
1 tsp. cumin seeds, mashed
1 tsp. oregano
1 stick canela or cinnamon
3 cloves, crushed
1 sprig thyme
1/2 cup apply cider vinegar
1 1/2 cups water
1 tbsp. brown sugar
1 1/2 tsp. salt

Remove the stems, the seed and the veins from all of the ancho chiles and from 5 of the chipotles. Toast the anchos and the 5 chipotle chiles (or use the hot oil method described on page 100). Soak the toasted ancho chiles and the 5 chipotles in hot water (*boiled water removed from the heat*) for about 30 minutes. Reserve this liquid from the soaking. Drop the 5 soaked chipotle chiles and all of the ancho chiles into a blender or food processor and pulse 2 or 3 times.

Then, add all the roasted tomatoes and 1 cup of the reserved soaking liquid to the processor. Purée until relatively smooth. Meanwhile, put the olive oil in a soup or stock pot and heat it. Add the next 7 ingredients (garlic, bay, cumin, oregano, cinnamon, cloves, and thyme) and stir them in the oil until they are hot. Add the chile paste from the processor to the pot and stir into the spices. Then add the 1/2 cup of apple-cider vinegar, the fresh water, the brown sugar and salt. Add all of the remaining chipotle chiles. *They can be used dry or oil roasted before they dropped in the broth.* Simmer for about 45 minutes or longer.

Remove from the heat and transfer to other containers. Make sure that you evenly distribute the chipotles to all of the containers. You can leave this chipotle en adobo in the refrigerator for several weeks, or you can place in smaller containers and freeze it. Your friends will love a small jar.

<u>*How to use this adobo*</u>

- **Chop the chiles and add to soups with 1-2 tbsp adobo.**
- **Purée a small amount of the adobo and chiles, and add to the basic red or ancho sauces to add extra flavour and bite.**
- **Add one chopped chipotle and a tsp. of adobo to the green tomatillo salsa (page 35) for a unique taste.**
- **Add to mashed potatoes.**
- **Purée a half-cup of it to make a special hot sauce similar to Herdez's brand 'Bufalo Chipotle Salsa'. Add a little water to make it thinner.**

CHIPOTLE PURÉE

Here's the easiest chipotle recipe of all. Of course, it's called chipotle purée. Just make this and keep it in your refrigerator to add to soup or whatever else strikes your fancy. For those of you who need a hint, you can take a giant freshly baked potato and add a bit of sour cream to the top. Then, put a 1/2 tsp. of this purée on top of the sour cream. Mmmm!

can of chipotles in adobo

Take a can of chipotles in adobo and purée in a food processor or blender. The resulting mixture can be substituted anywhere a recipe calls for whole canned chipotles. Roughly one teaspoon of the purée is equivalent to one whole chipotle. The purée can be added to salsas, to stews, soups and many other dishes for that marvelous smoky flavour.

TOMATO–CHIPOTLE SALSA

Chipotle chiles add a wonderful earthy flavour to any salsa. Here are a few examples, and then we are certain that your own imagination will take over. First, a tomato based mixture.

4 tomatoes

4 cloves garlic, peeled

1 onion, cut in large sections

1 chipotle chile—canned in its adobo sauce

2 tbsp. lime juice

1 tbsp. canola or olive oil

10 or so sprigs of cilantro

1 tbsp. fine red wine vinegar

Roast the tomatoes, garlic and onion in a small oven or on a grill until they are slightly charred. Drop into a mixing bowl and cover with clear wrap and let everything cool for a few minutes. In blender or food processor combine all ingredients. Remember to go easy and pulse lightly in order to make a chunkier salsa. Makes about 2 cups. It lasts 3-4 days in the refrigerator, but will be eaten long before then.

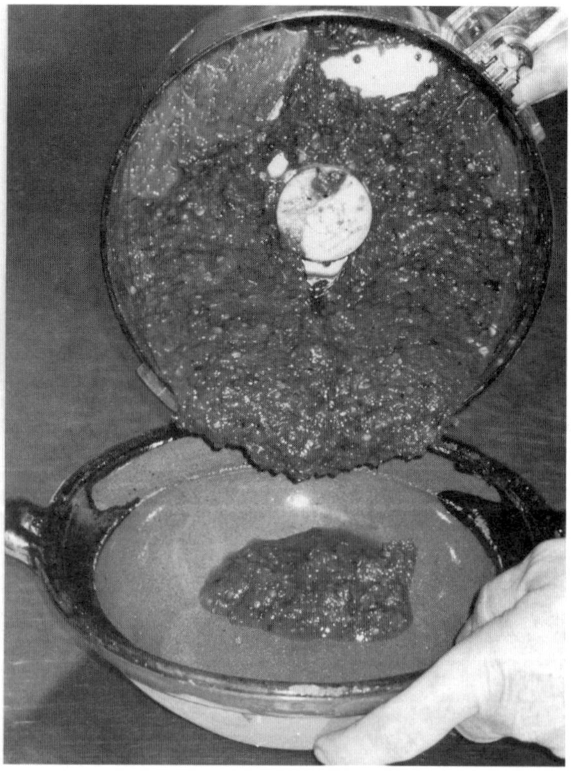

TOMATILLO–CHIPOTLE SALSA

This tasty salsa combines chipotles with tomatillos. It's delicious, and we also think that its colour is marvelous. On cold winter days, the very colour of this salsa helps you think you are warm.

8 tomatillos— husked and washed

4 cloves garlic, peeled

1/2 onion, cut in chunks

1/2 cup cilantro, chopped

2 canned chipotles in adobo

2 tbsp. ground cumin

2 tbsp. brown sugar, pilon, or honey

Roast the tomatillos, garlic and onion in a broiler or frypan with no oil. Remove the garlic and onion when brown. Broil the tomatillos until they are soft and turn yellow. Make sure that you turn them frequently. Place the tomatillos, garlic, onion and other ingredients in a blender or food processor. Blend to desired consistency, but chunky is best. You can add a bit of fresh water if you want to make it a little thinner. Makes about 1 1/2 cups.

Stuffed chipotles are a specialty in Puebla and Oaxaca. They are delicious. Moritas (a redder version of the chipotle) are soaked in milk, stuffed with a creamy white cheese, dipped in a light batter and fried. Often they're served beside a bed of lettuce. Yummy!

FIERY CHIPOTLE SALSA

The next salsa is for those of you who want to experience the full 'fire' of the chipotle. In fact it's called Fiery Chipotle Salsa and is based on one that is recommended by Reed Hearon in his book Salsa. Here's your chance to try dried chipotles at their best. Hearon recommends that you use this salsa with chips, scrambled into eggs, or just spooned onto roasted chicken or fish, accompanied by a shot of single-malt scotch. Well, alrighty then! We've used it as a barbecue sauce for salmon and halibut steaks with mouthwatering effects!

3 dried chipotle chiles

1 cup hot water

1 white onion— sliced and pan roasted

8 cloves garlic— pan roasted

1 tbsp. sherry vinegar

1/4 teaspoon ground cumin

1/4 tsp. dried Mexican oregano— toasted

1 tbsp. olive oil

1/2 tsp. salt (*optional*)

In a heavy skillet over medium heat toast the chiles until brown and fragrant. Use the oil technique if they are especially dry. Allow them to cool, slit them open and remove seeds. Toss chiles into 1/2 cup of hot water and let them soak for *at least* 10 minutes. Combine the chiles, soaking water and remaining ingredients in a blender. Process at high speed until you have a lightly textured liquid. Add the remaining 1/2 cup water. Makes about 2 cups.

PINEAPPLE-CHIPOTLE SALSA

Chipotle complements fruit in a very unique way. It is hard to describe the unique pleasure that comes from the contrasting sharpness and bite of this chile against the taste of a juicy and cool fruit. Although there are many salsa and fruit combinations, here's an interesting one to try. This fruity combination is great with seafood, chicken or pork. And, not only that, it's perfect with Asian appetizers like spring rolls and gyozas.

1 cup fresh pineapple, diced

1 cup peeled apple, diced

1/4 cup red bell pepper, seeded and diced

1 chipotle—from can of chipotle en adobo, cut into small pieces

2 tbsp. orange juice

1/4 cup cilantro, chopped

1 tbsp. brown sugar, pilon, or honey

Sauté pineapple in fry pan until brown. Add remaining ingredients and mix. Makes about 2 cups.

CHIPOTLE MAYO

Want to spice up that old standby mayonnaise? Here's how! Serve this exotic dressing with seafood or as a dip for shrimp or just add it to your favorite salad. It's also great as a topping for cooked cauliflower.

1/2 cup mayonnaise

1/2 cup yogurt or sour cream

2 canned chipotle chiles in adobo, chopped

or 2 teaspoons chipotle purée

Mix all ingredients and refrigerate before serving.

CHIPOTLE CREAM SAUCE

This versatile cream sauce is hot. It's from a 1994 Chile Pepper Magazine recipe credited to Chef Zeke Lambert of the restaurant "Lambert's of Taos". 'He recommends that this sauce be served with grilled meats and seafood.

6 shallots, peeled

1 large carrot, peeled and diced

1 to 2 tbsp. vegetable oil

2 to 4 canned chipotle chiles in adobo sauce

1/4 cup white wine

3 cups heavy cream *or* mixture of 1 1/2 cup cream and 1 1/2 cups chicken stock

Roast the shallots in an oven until tender and browned. Sautée the carrot in the oil until tender. Add the shallots, chipotles and the wine and simmer for a minute. Then add the cream, raise the heat and cook until the sauce has been reduced by one half. Place mixture in a blender or food processor and puree. Strain the mixture to produce a smooth sauce. Makes about 1 cup.

CHIPOTLE DRESSING

- 1 canned chipotle with about
- 1 tbsp. of adobo sauce or 2 tsp. chipotle puree
- 3 cloves garlic, peeled
- 6 sprigs cilantro
- 1/2 cup white vinegar *or* seasoned rice vinegar
- juice of 1/2 lime
- 1/2 cup canola or olive oil
- 1 tsp honey

Chipotle can also spice up a light salad dressing. Just add a dollop to your own favorite vinegar and oil combination or try this simple recipe.

Blend chipotle, garlic, cilantro and vinegar in food processor or blender, slowly add oil, and lime juice and honey.

CHIPOTLE-ZUCCHINI

- 1 lb. of zucchini, peeled and cut into wedges
- 2 tbsp. cooking oil
- 1 medium size onion, chopped
- 4 cloves garlic, chopped
- 2 roma tomatoes, chopped
- 1 canned chipotle chile in adobo, chopped or 1 tsp. chipotle purée
- 1/2 cup sour cream
- parmesan cheese, grated for sprinkling on top

Now here's a way to add that exotic chipotle flavour to vegetables. This recipe uses zucchini but chipotle is also great with mashed potatoes, scalloped potatoes, cooked cabbage, rice, corn and beans.

Heat oil in frying pan and sauté onion and garlic. Cook until onion is soft. Add zucchini, tomatoes and chile. Cover and simmer until zucchini is slightly cooked but still crunchy. Remove from heat and stir in sour cream.
Serve topped with grated cheese. Makes enough for 4. For a variation, do this on the barbecue.

ALBONDIGAS (MEATBALLS) EN CHIPOTLE

Just about everything is made into a soup in Mexico—from a fungus that grows on corn (huitlacoche) to squash blossoms to garlic. One of our favorites is Sopa de Albondigas (Meatball soup). But while in Mexico City, we discovered a meatball recipe with chipotle that uses ground chicken, turkey, beef and pork in various combinations. We've included one recipe that features the flavour of mint. In Mexico, slices of hard boiled eggs are often cooked inside the meatballs.

4 cloves garlic, chopped
1/2 cup onion, chopped
1/2 cup cooked rice
2 tbsp. fresh mint, chopped
1 tsp. oregano
1 tsp. ground cumin
1 egg
1 lb. ground beef
1 lb. ground pork
1/2 cup pine nuts

Mix all ingredients together and form into small balls. Place meatballs in greased frying pan and cook until done. Add the following salsa.

SALSA DE CHIPOTLE

1 tbsp. olive oil
4 garlic cloves
1 can cooked tomatoes or 8 roma tomatoes chopped
1 1/2 cups chicken stock
3 canned chipotles en adobo sauce, chopped

Sauté garlic in oil. Add tomatoes, chicken stock and chipotles. Simmer until hot. Add meatballs to salsa and simmer for 10 minutes. Serve hot with rice, tortillas and salad.

My Notes About Chipotles

Putting Chiles By

A lot of time and effort has gone into developing ways to make the chile harvest last. Depending on the type of chile- you can freeze, can or pickle, dry or smoke.

Obviously some techniques are easier than others and some require the right climate.

The ways to store chiles

Fortunately, chiles can be stored in many different ways! By far, the easiest technique is freezing, and we prefer it because it's convenient for keeping freshly roasted chiles. But you may want to experiment with other methods of preserving.

The earliest storage was accomplished by *drying chiles in the sun*. People learned that adding a little liquid to dried peppers produced a delicious version— not too dissimilar from the fresh version. Of course, they also discovered that dried chiles had acquired many unique and wonderful qualities.

The easiest way to dry is to let the chiles dry on the plant or to lay the chiles on a cloth (sackcloth) covering flat on the ground. Some people invest a little more time in this process and create beautifully decorative ristras by stringing the chiles together. We are not experts at this, and if you are really interested you should check out a book like the Whole Chile Pepper Book which provides instructions. We noticed that many mail order companies are now willing to send ristras at very high prices. Check out the internet.

The *Mexica* peoples learned how to *smoke fatter chiles* for long term preservation, and their ancient techniques are still widely used in Mexico. As we told you earlier, there are now commercialized versions of a smoking process. Smoking allows access to chiles all year round— but it also adds a wonderful exotic flavour that is highly valued in its own right. Personally, you can be very inventive if you own a smoker and if you have access to large quantities of fat fleshy chiles.

The fatter-fleshed chiles are also perfect for *pickling or canning*. All it takes is a deep pot and a willingness to invest in some canning jars, to create 'chiles en escabeche'. We explained most of these rules earlier on page 46. But, be sure to follow the safe rules for canning if you do this. It is a safe method for storage when done correctly— but deadly when one doesn't follow the rules exactly.

Freezing

Whole Chiles

Perhaps you'd like to roast and clean a large quantity of whole chiles for future use. Fortunately, roasted chiles freeze well and can be kept for several months when stored properly. They should be kept in a tightly sealed container— either a freezer bag or plastic carton with an air-tight top. And, you can actually wrap them in a way which lets you use a few at a time. We have gathered all of these tips and put them into the tip side-bar which follows.

For Chile Strips

Basically, follow the same process as for whole chiles. Obviously chiles should be peeled and cleaned first. To avoid clumping during freezing— *separate* the strips as you wrap them. If you plan to use them all at once (chopping or purée) don't worry about separating them.

Chopped Chile

Ice trays are handy for storing *chopped* chile. Spray the little cubes with a small amount of cooking oil and place one or two tablespoons of chopped chile in each section. The frozen chile cubes are easy to remove individually and they are just the right size for many recipes. Just be sure the tray is covered and tightly sealed to avoid freezer burn.

Other methods of preserving

If you're interested in the other ways of preserving chiles it becomes a bit more complicated. For example small, fleshy chiles like jalapeños can be pickled or canned in which case they become jalapeños '*en escabeche*.' But these are also available at the market at reasonable prices. Flat and fleshy chiles can also be smoked. Once again, its the jalapeño that's often processed in this way. When smoked it's called a chipotle chile and its rich, earthy flavour is wonderfully addictive.

Canning/Pickling

If you are familiar with the basic steps of canning/pickling and preserving, you can put aside some chiles or salsas for those dark days of winter. Chiles are low in acid, and this means that canning recipes require acid to stop spoilage. Most recipes call for adding white vinegar with a 5% acetic acid content. When you find a pickling recipe—follow it exactly.

We did provide 2 simple canning recipes (jalapeños en escabeche, and green chile salsa) for those of you who own canning equipment and enough time to do this (see page 44). Most of us will have to be content to buy the commercial versions of chiles en escabeche.

Smoking/Curing:

Smoking and drying chiles requires even more equipment and time than canning does, and it is definitely for dedicated aficionados. However, people with the luxury of space, time and equipment can experiment with smoking. We recommend a copy of Jacqueline Higuera McMahan's book Chipotle Chiles, or a visit to the library in search of a copy of Chile Pepper Magazine from October 1992. It contains an the article by Dr. Paul W. Bosland, (Agronomy and Horticulture Department at New Mexico State University) called "*The Chipotle, Mystery- Solved at Last!*"

Summaries of this article are also widely available on the internet.
One site is http://neptune.netimages.com/~chile/chipotles.html at the time of printing.

Freezing Tips

• To use just a few chiles at a time here's how to store them.

—Lay out a long sheet of plastic wrap. At one end, cover with wax paper and top with 1 or 2 chiles.

—Roll plastic wrap over the chiles a few times, then lay down another piece of wax paper with chiles and roll as before.

—Continue the same way with as many chiles as you wish. place total package inside a freezer bag.

—To use, just unwrap the outer edges of the plastic wrap covering the chiles you want to use.

• Frozen chiles can become bitter when not properly stored or if they are stored for too long.

•They should probably be used within 6 months. Be sure they're completely covered and sealed during freezing.

Storing in refrigerator

• Keep the chile in a bowl. the natural oils separates from the flesh.

• Be sure to use the liquid from stored chiles in your final recipe.

Chile Complements

Chiles can stand alone, so to speak. But they're usually combined with other ingredients to make salsas, rellenos, or smooth sauces. Here's a description of the most common chile complements with some notes on how to use them.

Markets on wheels (Tianguis en ruedas) are set up in most neighbourhoods of Mexico City. At least once a week, fresh ingredients are within walking distance of every home.

In Mexico, almost all neighbourhoods have a local tortilla shop which sells fresh corn tortillas. Tianguis en rueda have at least one booth which sells fresh tortillas made from all types of corn, in different shapes and sizes, and filled with delicious stuffings.

New Spain (Mexico) has contributed an astounding number of foods to the world— tomatoes, squash, beans, corn, peanuts, vanilla, chocolate and chiles. Many of these foodstuffs were growing in Mexico when the Spaniards landed at Vera Cruz in late1518. And as wave after wave of foreign explorers crossed their lands, Mexicans became highly adept at incorporating new elements into their cooking. Flour, cilantro, cream, and beef were quickly adapted in new and innovative ways. Mexicans speak proudly of the strengths they've gained from their cultural *mestizaje* (mes-tee-zah-hey). In this chapter, we discuss some of the ingredients regularly used with chile peppers in Mexican cooking.

Tomatoes:

We use *plum* or *roma* tomatoes in southwestern and Mexican cooking. The full flavour of ripe plum tomatoes complements the other ingredients nicely— and besides the tomatoes are almost always chopped up so presentation is not a big factor. There are generally fewer seeds, and the shape and size facilitate roasting.

We like to roast tomatoes before we use them— just plop them on the barbecue or on the fry pan along with the chiles. Roasting adds a richness to the flavour, especially if the skin is actually charred. We sometimes roast a bunch of tomatoes in advance and let them sit in a covered container in the refrigerator. Tomatoes can be skinned before use depending on the texture you want. For a chunky salsa, leave the skin on when you chop the tomato. For smoother and less chunky salsas peel or strain the tomato.

Tomatoes are just one of the many gifts from Mesoamerica to the rest of the world (along with chocolate, avocados, chiles, peanuts, and vanilla). Europeans thought the tomatoes were poisonous until they discovered how wonderfully the Aztecs and other tribes of the Americas used them. In the presidential palace on the Zocalo in Mexico City, there are wonderful murals by Diego Rivera. In one of these, he pays tribute to the products which ancient Mexico gave to the world.

Tomatillos:

Tomatillos are mistakenly called 'green tomatoes' in some cookbooks. Although they *are* distantly related to tomatoes, they're more closely related to a cape gooseberry. The tomatillo is one of the best kept secrets of Mexican and southwestern cooking. They are an enigma to many of us, but once you find out how easy they are to use they'll become a regular ingredient in your salsas.

The pronunciation of this vegetable is "*toe-ma-tee—yo*".

Unfortunately, they have several names in Spanish language cookbooks. In parts of Mexico, *tomatillos* are called *chiltomates* and they may also be called *tomates verdes*. Cooks aren't trying to confuse you by using these names since everyone is aware that a tomato is a *jitomate* in Mexico and a green tomato is a *jitomate verde*.

We're sure that you've seen tomatillos at the market. They're an odd green looking thing in a papery husk covering. The fruit inside is a yellowish-green with a sticky surface. Some versions have a hint of purple in the colour. Remove the husks and gently wash under cold water or let them sit for a few minutes in a bowl of cool water. There are a few recipes that use raw tomatillos, but they are almost always cooked.

Boiling tomatillos

Tomatillos are prepared in one of two ways, and each method produces a different flavour. The fast way is to put cleaned tomatillos in a saucepan and barely cover them with water. Bring the water to a boil and cook until they are soft and opaque. Let them cool and then put them and a small part of the cooking liquid (about 1/4 of the total) into a food processor for liquefying. This method produces a juicy and acidic base for salsas.

Roasting tomatillos

The other method of preparation is our favorite! We roast tomatillos on a barbecue, frying pan or in a broiler oven. The tomatillos take on a wonderful golden yellow colour and retain their solidity— thus producing a chunkier and sweeter salsa. To roast, simply wash and place them on a barbecue. They cook from the inside, and eventually the liquid inside heats up and starts to escape. When you notice that a thin liquid stream shoots out, or you see an 'oozing' of liquid turn them over until all sides are softened and slightly blackened. They can become dry if they are overcooked, so don't leave them on the heat for too long.

Once they are soft, place them in a bowl where they continue to cook and the juicy liquid collects in the bottom of the bowl. We generally cover a bowl with a clear wrap, and let the tomatillos stew in their own juices before we put them in the refrigerator. If covered, they will keep for a week or more. These roasted tomatillos are used the same way as the boiled ones. But, they produce a *chunkier salsa* and you might have to add a bit of additional liquid to thin the mixture. Ordinary water works for this thinning process, but you can be very creative and add your favorite liquid. Reed Hearon suggested that he liked to sip a single malt scotch with a chipotle tomatillo salsa, but you can go one better and add a dab of scotch, tequila or mescal directly to the tomatillos. We promise you, this is not a waste !

In the Mexican State of Guerrero, cooks save the papery husks of tomatillos and boil them in water. This 'flavoured' water is used to make the masa for tamales.

Onions

Onions are a must in the Mexican and Southwestern kitchen. Pick the finest you can find. For a mild, sweet flavour use white onions. For a stronger, hotter taste, Spanish onions are best. In Mexico, the Spanish onions are described by their colour (*morado,* i.e. purple). Once again, we recommend roasting them since this adds a rich, smoky flavour to the most ordinary salsas.

In the Yucatan, onion slices are very frequently marinated in mild vinegar and added as condiments to dishes. They also marinate the onion (usually Spanish) in a mixture of vinegar and the bitter juice of Seville oranges along with a halved habañero chile. Sweet oranges are prevalent in Canada and the USA, but you can sour the orange juice by adding a little white grapefruit juice or vinegar. There are some commercial bitter mixes that are good substitutes, and highly recommend for pouring on top of purple sliced onions.

Onion tips

• The method of preparing onions can greatly affect the final texture and flavour of a salsa.

•Roasting produces a wonderful flavour.

• White and red onions have different flavours.

• Some cooks add white onions to a blender/processor and purée them into a white creamy liquid. Other salsa ingredients are added to this mixture and only lightly processed. The result is a creamy salsa with a chunky texture.

Garlic

Garlic cloves are used in almost all salsas. It's worthwhile to seek out the freshest and the best. And, of course, we recommend you roast the cloves of garlic. It adds extra flavour and a creamy smoky texture to salsas. The garlic can simply be thrown onto a fry pan and darkened, or put in a toaster oven.

But there is one delicious way to roast a lot of garlic at one time. Take a *whole head of garlic,* and remove as much of the papery covering as you can. Then, cut the individual clove tips by slicing across the top of the whole cloves with a very sharp knife. Place this whole garlic, uncut side down, in a small counter top oven pre-heated to about 400°F. Cook it for about 40 minutes in total, but you should cover the garlic with a loose 'cap' of tin foil after the first 10 minutes. You can periodically drizzle oil or drop butter or high quality olive oil on the top of the garlic, and you can sprinkle spices (e.g. oregano is fantastic) while it bakes under the tin foil. Once it has cooked, let the garlic cool, and then carefully squeeze out individual cloves from their skin and add to your recipe. If you find that the garlic is too 'mushy' to squeeze out, then cook the next garlic for a little less time.

Since garlic is cheap when bought in bulk, we often roast whole batches of it at once. In fact, we did buy a trendy garlic roasting pan from an Italian specialty market. After we have roasted 20 or 30 garlic cloves, we drop all of the individual cloves into a fresh bottle and top it with a high quality olive oil. It does keep on the shelf for several weeks. It keeps longer in the refrigerator, but the olive oil must thaw a little before you can remove individual cloves for cooking.

The famous Tucson restaurant, El Charro sells a cookbook of house recipes, and they describe how they prepare garlic ahead of time. They simply use a garlic press and squish all of the cloves into a big jar. They then add fresh water to make a very concentrated liquid, which they spoon into many of their special recipes.

Garlic Tips

- **If garlic has been roasted, use about twice as much as the recipe suggests.**
- **You can roast garlic quickly in a microwave. A whole garlic is prepared as above (peel and slice the top) and then placed in the centre of microwave and cooked on high for 5 minutes or until soft.**
- **Save the garlic tips in a freezer bag, and add them to your stocks.**

Cilantro

Fresh cilantro (also called Chinese parsley or fresh coriander) is another essential companion for chiles. An interesting little journal called Petits Propos Culinaires contains an article by Elisabeth Labert Ortiz that describes fresh coriander in detail. As she points out, it has a very distinctive flavour and seems to be a taste that people either love or hate. She also notes that coriander did not reach the new world until after 1493, but that "all of Latin America took to using the green leaves with fish and seafood, meat and poultry, in salads and soups and as a garnish".

In Mexico, Ortiz says it is the most popular herb, and it is taken for granted that it is an indigenous plant. She can find no evidence that the Spaniards brought it to Mexico, and she suspects that Filipinos actually introduced it. How ever it arrived— it became essential.

We can't imagine Mexican food without cilantro but if it is one of those tastes that you don't like— then leave it out of the recipes.

Some soups or broths call for a bunch of cilantro to be tied and dropped in during the cooking. It is removed and discarded when dishes are done. This is an especially common practise when cooking seafood.

Cilantro is now available everywhere. Purchase the freshest and greenest you can find.

Cilantro should be added to your recipe at the last moment so that it doesn't really cook and lose its shape, colour or flavour. Or, you can serve it as a condiment to be added individually according to people's preferences. Some cooks just pinch off the leaves when it is a condiment, but if you are adding it to a soup or stew then it is worthwhile to add both stems and leaves.

Cilantro Tips

- **When you get cilantro home, rinse it and place the bunch standing in a glass of water.**
- **Cover the leaves with a plastic bag and secure it with a rubber band around the lip of the glass of water. It keeps this way in refrigerator for several days.**
- **Check it periodically and remove the leaves that are yellowing or turning black.**
- **Add to hot sauces at the last minute.**
- **Generally, do not add to dishes if the dish is to be cooked.**
- **If you add cilantro at the start of cooking, tie the leaves together and remove it after everything is done.**
- **Add cilantro after cooking all other ingredients.**

Avocado

Avocados are used to make *guacamole* and are also added to other chile salsas. When selecting avocados at the market, choose ones that are a darkish green, without blemishes and which are soft but still firm to the touch. A ripe avocado has a *springy* flesh; if you push your finger *lightly* down it *gives* and then *regains* its shape. You can buy 'hard' avocados and let them soften at home. We have noticed that ripe avocados are rarely available in the big supermarkets, and we usually have to purchase ahead of time and store them in a paper bag in a dark place. They ripen in a day or two. Our daughter explained to us that the produce manager where she worked in a large supermarket would test avocados and remove those that had any 'springy' quality. The best ones ended up in the garbage.

For those of you interested in trivia, the term avocado comes from the Aztec word for testicle– 'ahuacatl'.

Limes

Limes are an important ingredient in many salsas. In fact, in Mexico they're used in the same way we might use salt and pepper. They're squeezed onto everything from soup to nuts. In fact, Mexicans use a lime slice to rub the top of beer cans.

In Mexico fresh limes are so common that they are *grouped* and sold by size— not so north of the border where we buy whatever size happens to come our way. Small ones are highly prized, and household cooks choose specific sizes to make particular salsas. Whatever the size, a dish of sliced limes is a great condiment with salsas.

Lime Tips

• Limes in Mexico are sweeter than the ones we buy.

• In other parts of North America, Mexican limes are called key limes.

• This explains why homemade Key Lime Pies never taste the same as the ones you eat on vacation.

• The limes generally available to us are Persian limes.

• Lemons are not used in Mexico.

Tortillas

There are two types of tortillas— flour and corn. Both are widely available in all areas— but unfortunately the packaged ones bear very little resemblance to the 'real thing'.

In Mexico corn tortillas are usually made with white corn (*maiz*). The kernels are soaked in a lime and water mixture (*cal*) to soften the outer skin. The softened kernels (*nixtamal*) are placed in special bowls with decorative holes in the bottom, and water is poured over the top to rinse away the powdered *cal* or limestone.

Rinsed *nixtamal* is ground by hand on a small platform made of volcanic rock called a *metate*, and this *masa* is formed into golf-sized balls which are flattened and heated on a flat cooking pan called a *comal*. Of course, modern grinding methods are more prevalent and pre-mixed dried masa is the norm. Recently, there were major scandals in Mexico when the production of masa became a monopoly industry. There is also a great anxiety about the national subsidy for masa which is gradually being removed. The price of this basic food has skyrocketed.

Ideally tortillas are eaten absolutely fresh, hot off the grill (*comal*). Most restaurants and food vendors in Mexico prepare and heat tortillas *as needed* for their customers and as meals are ordered. Tortillas that are absolutely fresh have an unbeatable taste.

Blue corn tortillas are also available in Mexico. The best corn tortillas have a grainy texture, are not too white, and a have full, earthy flavour.

Unfortunately, the tortillas we buy here have more in common with rubber than corn. There are no pre-packaged brands of corn tortillas that we would recommend.

Make your own

Believe it or not, you'll probably be better off buying a bag of *Maseca* (corn flour tortilla mix) and making tortillas in your kitchen. We'll tell you a bit more about this below.

When it comes to *flour* tortillas, nothing compares with those from the Sonoran region of Mexico and Arizona where they have been perfected. The most delicious ones are made with *lard*, but even 'diet–conscious' flour tortillas have a high proportion of other oil. It is possible to find whole wheat and other types of flour tortillas— but these are not common in Mexico and are rarely used in authentic kitchens within Mexico. Strong tasting oils (e.g. olive) change the taste of tortillas and are not to a traditionalist's liking.

Modern nutritionists encourage poorer countries to adopt corn as an ideal food source. However, in some of these countries, they strip and crush the kernels with powerful grinders creating a corn meal, which is different in quality and food value from that processed in Mexico. In Mexico the use of lime adds an important mineral to the corn, which in turn complements the amino acids. If you're buying tortillas avoid the dark yellow ones. These have probably been made with a harder corn kernel that has been crushed by machine. They are less tasty and definitely less nutritious.

A new fast food trend from California uses the flour tortilla as a wrap. Often, these tortillas are flavoured and come in different colours. We find it odd that this new fast food is described as low in fat when flour tortillas actually contain about the same amount of fat as bread. Unfortunately, the '*wraps*' themselves are often bland and are stuffed with even blander fillings. A rather poor imitation of a burrito.

There are over 50 types of corn cultivated in Mexico but few them resemble the sweet yellow corn we consume in the United States and Canada. Many Mexicans use yellow corn to feed livestock.

To make corn tortillas, carefully follow the instructions on the bag of masa harina (*Maseca* Brand) to make a masa dough. 'Tear off' a piece of the dough about the size of a golf-ball, roll it in your hands a few times to smooth the surface, and then uniformly flatten it to about 1/8" thick. This flattening can be done by hand, or by pressing the masa lightly between two boards, or even using a rolling pin.

Placing kitchen baggies or wax paper on the top and bottom of the masa makes it easier to handle during this pressing. Tortillas come in all shapes and sizes in Mexico, but you will probably find it best to make round tortillas about 4" (10 cm) across. The golf-size ball produces a 4" tortilla.

After the masa has been shaped and pressed to a thickness of 1/8" (.3 cm), the flattened masa is placed on a very hot griddle and cooked lightly for 15-20 seconds. *There is a trick to laying a tortilla on a hot grill*— lay the masa flat on your palm so that part of it '*drapes*' over the edge of your hand (opposite your thumb). Then, with your palm facing up, allow the bottom edge of the tortilla to catch the hot surface and stick slightly— and, in one slow turning motion, 'roll' your palm *up and away* from the griddle. The tortilla should fall gently into place. Let it heat for about 7-10 seconds and use your finger to lightly poke the middle of the cooking tortilla . It should puff up in the middle! When it puffs, turn the tortilla over and cook the other side. The tortilla is done when both sides have puffed and there are a few *light* brown spots on both sides. Use only a little oil in the pan to prevent sticking because too much oil will prevent the tortilla from cooking properly.

The sign of a perfect tortilla is the shape, and the fact that the masa puffs in the middle when the first side is cooking. Place the cooked tortillas in a wrapped clean 'cloth' or tea towel and keep it covered until use. A high quality tortilla is actually quite white!

Tortilla Tips

- **The rule of thumb for decent tortillas- *make them at home!***
- **For flour tortillas, buy a bag of *MASA de TRIGO* (wheat flour). Add a solid shortening (e.g. Crisco) as well as water and a little salt.**
- **For corn tortillas, use MASA HARINA. There is no substitute, since corn meal does not have the cal which makes corn masa unique.**
- **Add only warm water and a bit of salt.**

Queso or Cheese

We hope that the North American Free Trade Agreement (TLC in Mexico) will eventually make Mexican cheeses more widely available in Canada and the USA. In Mexico most cheeses are white, light bodied and used sparingly– a perfect complement to tortillas and salsas.

There are vastly different preferences about 'which cheese' and 'how much cheese' should be used in Mexican cooking. In Southern Arizona and Northern Sonora, many dishes are smothered with generous amounts of a golden yellow cheese— usually longhorn or colby. In California, many dishes are sprinkled with sour cream instead of cheese. In central Mexico, cheese is used more sparingly, and it is almost always a white, slightly–acidic cheese from Oaxaca or Chihuahua.

At the great risk of oversimplifying, we'll provide a few general tips about using cheese or dairy products. There are essentially three ways that cheese is used in 'chile cooking'. Some dishes call for a cheese that *MELTS* evenly. Many simple tortilla dishes (e.g. nachos, quesadillas) are not much more than tortillas and a smoothly melted cheese. Other dishes call for *SPRINKLING* small 'chunks' of a soft crumbly cheese on top of an assembled dish. The wonderful simplicity of black beans sprinkled with a soft white cheese can't be beat. Finally, some dishes use a *THIN COVERING* of a thick cream. The wonderful dish, Chiles en Nogada depends on a final coating of a rather rich dairy cream mixed with crushed walnuts.

Some cheeses are reasonable substitutes for the Mexican product. *Feta cheese* is a reasonable substitute for a soft white 'queso fresco' that is sprinkled on top of beans and other dishes. We have also used a big curd *ricotta cheese, mixed it with a little parmesan* and then added a little bit of cumin and oregano to create an acceptable substitute for queso fresco. *Parmesan* is a reasonable substitute for a harder type of Mexican cheese called *queso cotija*. So is the Italian favorite, *asiago*.There really is no substitute for Oaxacan cheese, but we have learned to live with a *white farmer's cheese*, a *string* cheese, a *longhorn*, or a *colby*. The *crema fresca* is unique, but a reasonable substitute is a mixture of 1/2 sour cream and 1/2 heavy whipping cream (35%). You can also mix 1/2 cup of whipping cream and 1/2 cup of buttermilk to produce an approximation of a Mexican *crema fresca*. We often just use a plain white yogurt instead of the *crema fresca*.

Cheese Substitutes

- **Mexican Queso Fresco – Feta, Parmesan–Flavoured Ricotta**
- **Mexican Queso Cotija – Parmesan, Asiago**
- **Oaxacan Queso – Colby, Farmers, Longhorn, Soft Cheddar, String cheese**
- **Crema Fresca– A mixture of 1/2 whipping cream and 1/2 buttermilk**

Piloncillo.

A popular sweetener in Mexican cooking is a coarse sugar cane product called *piloncillo* (pee-lon-see-yo) or *pilon* (pee-lon). In southern parts of Mexico it is more often called *panela* (pan-el-la). It is sold in cone shapes of various sizes, and is a dark brown colour. It is widely available in Latino stores in different sizes, but we suggest you buy the smallest size which is exactly the right amount for Carmen's Salsa (page 114). If you buy the bigger sizes, it must be 'broken' into pieces before it is melted in a liquid.

Do not use white sugar under any circumstance. An acceptable alternative for pilon is 'demera' natural brown sugar because of its crystalline texture. Malt sugars, which are darkened with molasses, are semi-acceptable.

A dark golden honey also produces adequate results.

Complementary Spices and Seasonings

Several spices and seasonings go naturally with chiles, and you should always have a supply of the following:

Oregano

Mexican oregano is often used in salsas. It is coarser and broader then Greek oregano, but in a pinch use the Greek variety. We suggest *toasting* it lightly before adding to a recipe. You do this in a dry frying pan. Heat for 15– 30 seconds until it changes colour. Remove immediately.

Whole Cilantro Seed

This round seed is crushed and added to many salsas. It too can be lightly toasted in a frying pan before it is crushed. Do not toast too long as it blackens quickly.

Cumin (Comino) Seed

This is another unique seed that is crushed and added to many salsas. It too can be roasted lightly before crushed and added to recipes.

Bay Leaf

Whole bay leaves are often roasted and crushed before adding to recipes.

Cinnamon Bark

Whole cinnamon is a common ingredient in many salsas. McCormick's and company have a true Ceylon canela that is similar to the Mexican version of cinnamon.

Regional Specialties

This list of spices has been kept to an absolute minimum, and there are always wonderful results with the simplest list of ingredients. Having said that, many other spices from Mexico and the Southwest add delightful flavour, and are distinctive ingredients in dishes. Some of these are widely used (e.g. *epazote*), but others are regional (e.g. *acuyo* or *hoja santa* from coastal Vera Cruz).

Epazote

Fresh epazote stems and leaves are essential to 'bean pots' throughout Mexico, and this relative of wormwood grows wild across most of North America. These other spices are found only in the fresh markets of the streets and even more difficult to bring back to Canada or the US. Customs regulations forbid the importation of plants.

Vera Cruz has an incredible culinary richness and an amazing assortment of unique spices. It is also a place of fantastic music and dance!

Epazote is a very important ingredient in southern Mexican cooking, but it is very hard to find. It grows easily, and in fact is considered a nuisance weed by many people. It is a great complement for black beans.

Hoja Santa is used for making special tamales, but you can also improvise by using a little bit of fennel or anise seed to provide the licorice quality in any recipe you find.

Chile Charts

We have tried to keep this book simple, and have emphasized how chiles are used in general ways. However, some people are interested in cross-classifying chile types and in trying to understand how they relate to each other. In some recipes, a rather exotic chile might be called for and you may need to substitute for it. We created the following classification charts to classify chiles in general and list them beside their common equivalents.

The chiles are categorized into Fresh Chiles (2 pages) and Dried Chiles (2 Pages). Each type of chile is described by its general characteristics (size, heat level and use). Then, the chiles which are commonly available in Canada and the United States are described on the left hand side of the table (first column). The third column lists the most common Mexican names for these chiles and the fourth column lists chiles which are very closely related.

The point to remember is that each of the chiles in each row are used in similar ways.

Fresh Chiles

Most fresh chiles are bright green, but it is possible to find fresh ones that are red, orange, yellow, purple, or even a rich chocolate.

Characteristics
Small size chiles, shape is round, oval or pellet-like. Very picante.

General Uses:
Fresh Salsa, Pickled, Raw

Canada / USA	How is it used?	Mexico
Piquin *Extremely rare outside of Mexico*	*Salsa* *Pickled*	**Piquin** **Chile de Montaña**

Characteristics
Small, elongated chiles, thicker flesh, 'pungent' and moderate heat

General Uses:
Fresh Salsa, Pickled, Raw, Cooked salsa
Occasionally Stuffed

	Canada / USA	How is it used?	Mexico	Closely related Mexican Chile
	**Serrano**	*Fresh Salsa* *Pickled*	**Serrano** **Altamira** **Cotaxla** **Cuauhtémoc** **Panuco** **Tampiqueño**	Fresh Chile de arból (cola de rata)
	**Jalapeño**	*Fresh Salsa* *Pickled* *Stuffed* *Cooked Salsa*	**Jalapeño** **Cuarasemeño** **Candelaria** **Huachinango** **Gordo, Jarocho** **Papalonpan** **Pinateco** **Peludo** **Rayada** **Xalapeño**	Catarina Guero (Caloro, Cristal, Hungaro) Largo (Carricillo) Ixcatic

Characteristics

Longer, relatively thinner walls, 'slightly bitter' and mild heat

General Uses:
Rajas, Stuffed, Fresh and Cooked Salsas, Stews

Canada / USA	How is it used?	Mexico	
Anaheim Chile Verde New Mexico (Hatch, Chimayo,Big Jim)	*How is it used? Rajas Stuff Stew Salsa*	**Verde de Norte Magdalena Chile para rellenar**	*Closely related Mexican Chile* Chile de Agua
Chilaca **Note: rare outside of Mexico, and is 'longest' green chile**	*How is it used? Salsa Stew*	**Chilaca (chile para deshebrar, Cuerillo)**	

Characteristics

Wide, broad at top, 'slightly bitter', and very mild heat

General Uses:
Rajas, Stuffed, Fresh and Cooked Salsas, Stews, Moles

Canada / USA	How is it used?	Mexico
Poblano **Note: named Pasilla in parts of USA and Canada**	*How is it used? Rajas Stuff Salsa Stews*	**Poblano Chorro Chile para rellenar Esmeralda Gordo Jaral Joto Miahuateco Pasilla verde**

Characteristics

Round, bright colours, very likely to be hot

General Uses:
pickled, raw, some salsas

Canada / USA	How is it used?	Mexico	
Manzano	*How is it used? Pickled Raw*	**Manzana Caballo Canario, Cera Chamburato Ladino, Perón Rocoto**	*Related Mexican Chile* Bola (Bolito, Bolundo) Chilhuacle (Amarillo, Negro ó Rojo)
Habanero, Scotch Bonnet **Note: hottest fresh chile you will find**	*How is it used? Cooked Salsa Fresh Salsa Pickled*	**Habanero**	

Dried Chiles

Most are a red or rusty red, but the colours range from tan to black

Characteristics	General Uses
Naturally Dried, Reddish, Small and Round, and very picante	Seasoning, Adobo, Recado, Salsa

Canada / US name	How is it used?	Mexican name	Closely related Mexican Chile
Chiltepin, Piquin, Tepin **Note: Gary Nabhan claims the chiltepin started it all. It is a very trendy chile in southwest US.**	Season Adobo Recado Salsa	**Piquín, Amash Chile de monte, Chile de perro Chile piliento,Chilillo Chiltepin, Diente de Tlacoache Enano, Gachupín Pulga, Quimiche Tichusmín**	Pico de Paloma Tepín (Canica, Tempenchile, Pulga) Simojovel (Comapeño)

Characteristics	General Uses
Naturally dried, red, small and elongated with pointy end, usually quite picante	Season, Adobo, Recado, Cooked Salsa, Fresh Salsa

Canada / US name	How is it used?	Mexican name	Closely related Mexican Chile
Chile Japonesa Chile de Arbol	Season Adobo Recado Cooked salsa Fresh salsa	**Chile de árbol seco (Chile bravo, puya) Seco de costa serrano seco**	Costeño

Characteristics	General Uses
Naturally Dried Wider, colours from rust red to dark, can be hot. *These are dried Poblanos*	Season, Adobo, Recado, Salsa, Raja, Stew, Stuffed, Pickled

Canada / US name	How is it used?	Mexican name	Closely related Mexican Chile
Ancho **Note: this chile is sold in 'grades'. It has a wonderful raisin-like smell. The top quality has an almost transparent quality against a light. Mulato is essential to Mole**	Season Adobo, Recado Salsa Stuffed Raja, Stew Pickled	**Ancho (Chilacate, Chile de Guisar, Chino, Chinito, Colorado, Esmeralda, Flor de pabellón, Morelia)** **Mulato (Chocolate)**	Pasilla de Oaxaca

Characteristics

Naturally Dried, long, reddish, not usually hot
Dried versions of Anaheim or New Mexico Chiles

General Uses:
Season, Adobo, Enchilada, Stews

Chile Colorado, New Mexico Red **Note: these are the famous Southwest US ristra chiles. Chiles are not hung to dry in Mexico**	*How is it used?* *Season* *Adobo, Recado* *Salsa* *Enchilada* *Stew, Mole*	**Seco del Norte** **(Largo colorado)** **Chile pasado**	*Closely related Mexican Chile* Mirasol, Guajillo Guazón (chilaca roja ancha) Puya,Chilcoxle Costeño amarillo
True Pasilla **Note: it is harder to find this very dark chocolate chile. It is essential for moles. It is a dried chilaca.**	*How is it used?* *Season* *Adobo, Recado* *Salsa* *Stew, Mole*	**Pasilla** **(Achocolatado, Negro, Pasilla de Mexico, Prieto)**	

Characteristics

Smoke Dried, very hot with a wonderful smoked fragrance

General Uses:
Season, Adobo, Stew, Salsa

Chipotle **Note: this is the tan version of the smoked chile. It was 'smoked by the Aztecs. It is usually a dried jalapeño.'**	*How is it used?* *Season, Adobo,* *Salsa, Stew* *Pickled*	**Chipotle** **(chipocle, chilpotle, chile ahumado, huachinango, tamarindo, meco)**	
Morita ***Note: this is the smaller reddish version of smoked chiles***	*How is it used?* *Season* *Adobo, Salsa* *Stew, Pickled*	**Morita (Chilaile)**	

Books, Web Sites, Hot Tips and Final Thoughts

LEARNING MORE ABOUT CHILE PEPPERS AND MEXICAN FOOD

Obviously, since our book is called Beginning with Chiles, we know that our book is just a starting point. It is an *introduction* to those chile peppers that you've seen in your market and have been dying to use.

But we also know that once you've mastered the techniques of roasting and peeling, and once you discover the unique flavour characteristics of each chile, you'll want to find more complex combinations and even create recipes of your own. You'll definitely want to try out *moles*, *pipians*, *adobos* and even more complex versions of *chiles en nogada*. When that time comes, we invite you to check out some of the excellent Mexican cook books we've gathered here. Here's a list of the books we like with a few comments about each.

RECOMMENDED BOOKS

THE BORDER COOKBOOK

By Cheryl Alters Jamison and Bill Jamison.
Foreword by Mark Miller.
The Harvard Common Press, Boston, Mass., 535 Albany St.,
Boston 02118
1995

Thankfully, there really are no borders when it comes to culture and cuisine. And the culinary result is well presented. The Border Cookbook introduces the hearty, flavourful food of Northern Mexico and the Southwestern U.S.A. It includes regional specialties like Tex-Mex, Sonoran, and New Mexican styles of cooking. This tradition of cooking doesn't use the number and variety of chiles as one finds in Southern Mexico. Here, the Anaheim, New Mexico, and jalapeño chiles reign supreme. And the tiny chiltepin, which still grows wild in New Mexico, Texas and Arizona finds its way into several recipes.

LA COCINA DE LA FRONTERA

By James W. Peyton
Mexican-American Cooking from the Southwest
Red Crane Books, 826 Camino de Monte Rey,
Santa Fe, New Mexico 87505
1994

Another book that concentrates on 'border' cuisine. It has an interesting chapter on the origins of Mexican American cooking and information about distinctive regional differences. James Peyton describes salsas de chile colorado as "the heart and soul" of Mexican American cooking. Check out his chapter on these 'master' salsas for useful details on how they're made and used.

BIENVENIDOS TO OUR KITCHEN
By Luis and Marilyn Peinado
Published by Pelican Publishing Company Inc, 1101 Monroe Street, Gretna, La. 70053, 1992

We did not realize how authentic this book was until we lived in Mexico City. It has very simple recipes which are clearly presented. This couple basically describe the regular and daily meals of Mexico. It also has very interesting little tips about how to use prepared ingredients in innovative ways (e.g. Doña Maria Mole Poblano sauce).

EL NORTE, THE CUISINE OF NORTHERN MEXICO
By James W. Peyton
Published by Red Crane Cooks, 826 Camino de Monte Rey,
Santa Fe, New Mexico 87501,
1990

An earlier book by the author of La Cocina de la Frontera with different recipes.

MEXICO, THROUGH MY KITCHEN WINDOW
by Maria A. de Carbia,
Edited by Helen Corbitt
Book first published in Spanish in 1961.
In English published by: Houghton Mifflin Co., Boston, Mass.

This is an older book that was originally published in Spanish. The recipes have been adjusted for Canadian and American use and the authors assume it is necessary to substitute Anaheim chiles for poblanos. Of course, you can substitute back to the original. But it is a very interesting collection, which describes the role of food in culture and provides an appreciation for lasting traditions of this type of food.

FLAVORS OF MEXICO
By Angeles de la Rosa and C Gandia de Fernandez,
Published by 101 Production, 834 Mission St.
San Francisco, Ca. 94103

This is a book adapted from two other Spanish language books– Cocina Mexicana by Gandia de Fernandez, (1972) and Especialidades de la Cocina Mexicana by Angeles de la Rosa (1975). It has excellent recipes with detailed explanations for the preparation of more difficult recipes.

PEPPERS, HOT and CHILE:
By Georgeanne Brennan and Charlotte Glenn
Published by Aris Books, 1621 5th St.,
Berkeley, CA 94710,
1988

The subtitle, A Cook's Guide to Chile Peppers from California, the Southwest, Mexico and Beyond describes the content. It is a solid overview of chiles and how they are used in cooking.

AUTHENTIC MEXICAN:
Regional Cooking From the Heart of Mexico
By Rick Bayless with Deann Groen Bayless
Published in 1987 by Wm. Morrow and Co., Inc.
105 Madison Ave., N.Y. 10016

This has a very nice collection of regional recipes from Mexico.

CHILE PEPPER BOOK:A fiesta of fiery, flavourful recipes
By Susan Belsinger and Carolyn Dille
Published by Interweave Press, Inc., 201 East 4th St.,
Loveland, Colorado 80537.
1994

If you want more information on chiles, this 90 page book features a chart of over 25 peppers– their names, pungency, description, uses and other related information These 2 women have carefully researched all their is to know about chile peppers and include such topics as Chiles around the World, in the Kitchen. If you want info on growing and cultivating chiles, check out the section called "in the Garden". A limited number of recipes but an interesting variety, clearly presented with good tips.

CHILES AND OTHER PEPPERS
By Johanna Younger and James Fisher,
Illustrated by Jane Brewster.
Originally published in London by Quarto Inc., The Old Brewery, 6 Blundell St., London, England 1994.
In the USA published by Sunset Publishing Corp. Menlo Park, Calif. from a series called The Gourmet Kitchen

Another book on chiles with over 30 recipes of a more international variety— over 30 of them. Info on how to grow, select and store chile.

EL PASO CHILE COMPANY'S TEXAS BORDER COOKBOOK
By W. Park Kerr and Norma Kerr
Published by William Morrow and Co. Inc., N.Y.
1992.

Here the accent is on Tex-Mex! And, it's one of our favorites! written by a mother and son team who also own and operate the El Paso Chile Company. Their innovative and always delicious recipes are based on solid Mexican and Southwestern traditions.

COYOTE CAFÉ
By Mark Miller published in 1989
By Ten Speed Press, Berkeley, and Ca.

Another by Mark Miller is the Great Salsa Book. Chile explorer Amal Naj says that when Miller talks about food, he "just doesn't describe the form...but rather recounts his sensory experiences."

<u>THE WHOLE CHILE PEPPER BOOK</u>
By Dave DeWitt and Nancy Gerlach
Little, Brown and Company
1990.

An in-depth introduction to the world of chile peppers by the people who started Chile Pepper Magazine. Colour pictures of peppers with information on heat scale, legend and lore and such esoteric data as botanical descriptions, horticultural history, and agricultural aspects. For those of you who really want to get into the details etc. of capsaicin plants. Also includes over 180 hot and spicy recipes.

<u>SALSA</u>
By Reed Hearon.
Published by Chronicle Books,
275 Fifth Street, San Francisco, CA 94103,
Distributed in Canada by Raincoast Books, 112 East 3rd Ave, Vancouver, B.C. VST 1C8, 1993.

We love this book by San Francisco chef Reed Hearon. The recipes are easy to follow and beautifully photographed. And, there are an interesting variety of salsas using a good cross section of chile peppers. This is a must for your salsa library.

Reed Hearon has several other books out including <u>La Parilla, the Mexican Grill,</u> recommended for descriptions of the chile based recados of Yucatan.

<u>THE CUISINES OF MEXICO</u>
By Diana Kennedy.
Published by Harper and Row,
1972.

One of the 'bibles' of traditional Mexican cooking– it is a fascinating book filled with personal anecdotes and intriguing bits of information. Not to mention the recipes which are classics (albeit somewhat daunting). Diana Kennedy lived in Mexico while her husband was New York Times correspondent there. She is a world renowned expert on classic Mexican cooking. We met her in Mexico City at a cookbook fair held during 1997 Fiesta de Centro Historico. There are several editions of this book. Be sure to get the latest. Another Diana Kennedy cookbook is called "<u>The Tortilla Book</u>" published in 1976 by Harper and Row. Once again interesting anecdotes with recipes based on this Mexican staple.

MY MEXICO
By Diana Kennedy.
Published by Clarkson N. Porter, Inc
201 E. 5th Street,
New York, NY 10022
1998

Another 'must have book' from Kennedy. "My Mexico" is a highly personal account of Kennedy's travels in Mexico, highlighted by intriguing stories of her culinary discoveries. Knnedy's obvious affection for Mexico along with her extensive knowledge of its cuisine make each recipe special. Some dishes are exotic– Estafado de Raya (Skate Stewed in Olive Oil); others are relatively simple– Lobster Mushroom Quesadillas. All are worth adding to your collection. This book is for Mexicophiles.

THE TASTE OF MEXICO
By Patricia Quintana.
Published by Stewart, Tabori and Chang, Inc.
1986.

Patricia Quintana is another guru of la Cocina Mexicana. An author, cooking teacher and restaurant consultant, she is one of the foremost authorities on her native cuisine. This book is a classic– the recipes are classified by region and complimented with the exquisite photographs of Ignacio Urquiza who also did the pictures for Mexico, The Beautiful and Frida's Fiestas. This book definitely takes you there!

CUISINE OF THE WATER GODS
By Patricia Quintana
published by Simon and Schuster, New York
1994.

Another by Ms. Quintana. This time she takes us on a tour of Mexico's coastline, sampling the best of each region's cooking and setting it in the context of local culture and traditions. Incredible! Delicious recipes and great stories about the food.

FAVORITE RECIPES FROM EL CHARRO CAFE
By Carlotta Dunn Flores
Published by El Charro Cafe, Tucson Arizona, 1989.

We include this tiny book only because El Charro Cafe is one of the oldest Mexican American restaurants in the U.S.A. and has been a personal favorite since the sixties. El Charro is famous for their carne seca and this little book includes a homemade substitute. They do the real thing by hanging the beef to dry each day in the sun. Carne seca is made with long green chiles. El Charro is said to have created the carne seca chimichanga.

<u>SOUTHWEST COOKING</u>
By Betty Crocker published by Prentice Hall
1989.

Surprisingly good collection of Southwestern recipes, easy to make. The book is worth the price just to learn how to make biscochitos.

<u>MEXICO THE BEAUTIFUL COOKBOOK</u>

Published by Collins of San Francisco

1991

One of the beautiful cookbook series, this version definitely lives up to its name with the beautiful photographs of Ignacio Urquiza. His pictures make you want to run to the kitchen and get at it. And the recipes, by Susanna Palazuelos, are excellent— identified by State, clearly written, easy to follow. The only problem of course is keeping this big, beautiful book in coffee table condition.

<u>SOUTHWEST THE BEAUTIFUL COOKBOOK</u>
Published by Collins of San Francisco,
1994.

Equally beautiful, this gives you an overview of southwestern cooking— as much fun to look at and read as to use.

<u>CHIPOTLE CHILE COOK BOOK</u>
By Jacqueline Higuera McMahan
published by The Olive Press,
P.O. Box 194, Lake Hughes, Ca. 93532,
1994.

We referred to this book in our chapter on chipotles. Jacqueline has a number of books out on Mexican cooking including one called <u>Red and Green Chile Cookbook</u>. Read the Chipotle Cookbook if you want to know how and where the chipotle thing began, how to 'smoke' your own, and because it has lots of great chipotle recipes.

<u>FOODS OF THE SUN</u>
By Anne Lindsay Greer,
Published by Harper and Row,
1986.

Southwestern recipes with a Southern accent– Texas, Louisiana. This is a no nonsense cook book for those of you who want to experiment a bit with chile peppers. Try the chutney recipes. Many of the great Mexican political leaders spent a time of exile in New Orleans, and there have always been interesting connections in food tradition along the Yucatan, Vera Cruz, New Orleans corridor. That's the basis for most of these recipes.

THE FEAST OF SANTA FE
by Huntley Dent
Published by Simon and Schuster,
1985 with new Fireside Edition in 1993.

Cooking of New Mexico. Lots of recipes for New Mexico chiles.

MEXICAN COOKING AT THE ACADEMY
By Vicki Barrios Schley and Angelo Villa
Published by The Cole Group
in 1985, revised in 1993.

This book comes from the California Culinary Academy and is an excellent introduction to Mexican cooking. Check out the section on canning chiles and salsas. It has fantastic how–to pictures.

A COOK'S TOUR OF MEXICO
By Nancy Zaslavsky
Published by St Martin's Griffin,
1995.

This relatively new book (a nominee for the prestigious James Beard Award) is terrific– especially if you're planning a trip to Mexico. And if you're not planning a trip, this book will make you want to take one. Nancy provides a coast–to–coast tour of Mexican food and her emphasis is on the food of the people. She talks to vendors, village bakers, home cooks about some of Mexico's best known dishes and includes wonderful anecdotal information about other activities. If you are going to Merida in the Yucatan, or to Oaxaca City, we recommend that you read this book first!

FOOD FROM MY HEART: **Cuisines of Mexico Real and Imagined**
Zarela Martínez
Published by MacMillan, USA
1992.

This book is highly recommended for its stories about the importance of food in Mexican culture. Marvellous personal anecdotes. To top it off, there is a collection of some pretty good recipes from Northern Mexico and the state of Jalisco. If you want to know why people fall in love with Mexico and its people– then buy this book.

CHILE PEPPER MAGAZINE

This magazine, was started by a group of chile lovers in Albuquerque, New Mexico and was sold to a large publisher in 1996. However, while browsing on the web, we discovered that the magazine has been sold once again. In any event, the older copies have some excellent recipes and the newer versions are always interesting to browse. It's available at most newsstands and contains chile news and recipes from around the world.

AND, IF YOU SPEAK SPANISH

EL ARTE DE COCINAR CON CHILE
by Arturo Lomeli
published by Grijalbo
1986 with a revised edition in 1991.

Dr. Lomeli, a psychologist in Mexico, is a dedicated student and expert on chiles. His little book is incredibly valuable for the information on the origins of chile. He is an obvious gourmet, and his book contains some delicious chile recipes.

LA COCINA MEXICANA
published by Editorial Clio and Fundacion Herdez,
1996.

This fascinating 10 part series of high quality periodicals traces the history of Mexican cuisine from pre-Hispanic days covering aboriginal, Mestizo, Spanish and French revolutionary influences with special editions on regional varieties, everyday food. Hopefully there are plans for a translation. The Fundacion Herdez— a chile processing and canning company in Mexico, sponsored the series of 10 books and has recently established a major food archive at the National Autonomous University of Mexico (UNAM).

Authentic regional recipes and information about Mexico is located at the Mexico Desconocido web site. This is the best and most authoritative travel magazine about Mexico. The best stuff is in Spanish, but they are kind enough to provide some English text too. Visit it at

http://www.mexdesco.com/

OTHER BOOKS ABOUT RELATED THINGS.

GATHERIN G THE D ESERT
By Gary Paul Nabhan
Published by University of Arizona Press, Tucson, Arizona
1985 (now in its 4th printing).

Gary Paul Nabhan, an ethnobotanist, is the associate director of the Desert Botanical Gardens in Phoenix. He was a driving force behind Native Seeds/SEARCH– a non profit organization that maintains seed banks of indigenous Southwestern plants. This is a fascinating book on plants native to the Sonoran desert, their origins and cultural significance for Native living there. An amazing writer and the illustrations are beautiful and informative. Going to Arizona? Buy this book!

PEPPERS: A story of hot pursuits.
Amal Naj,
Vintage Books (A Division of Random House)
New York, 1992

Naj set off on a journey to learn about chiles and it took him to all of the hot spots of the USA. He visited New Mexico, Texas and Louisiana and learned a great deal about the relationship between agribusiness and chile peppers. He went on an international search to Bolivia, Peru and Mexico in search of other chiles. A great little book.

INTERNET and WORLD-WIDE WEB SITES

Chileheads and web addicts seem to have combined addictions. There some amazing sites on the world wide web. The world-wide-web is an open medium, and anybody can put whatever they want on it. Consequently, there's a lot of useful information about chiles and Mexican food– *but*, there is also trash.

Chile aficionados have made great use of the internet to post amazing information. The sites are also linked to each other through a 'ring-network'. Go to any site and you will see links to many other places.

We've scouted some sites and we suggest that you focus on the following links.

This first site is highly recommended. It is the Chile Head site, and it is guaranteed to contain answers to anything you ever wanted to know about chiles. This webmaster must be the most dedicated chile-head in the entire world.

http://easyweb.easynet.co.uk/~gcaselton/chile/chile.html

Chile Pepper Institute Site

http://www.nmsu.edu/~hotchile/index.html

The Tabasco Chile Company site

http://www.tabasco.com/

Chile Heads Home Page

http://neptune.netimages.com/~chile/

Canadian on–line source of hot stuff

http://www.hotpursuits.com/

A detailed address and *phone number*–site for all types of Southwestern and Mexican food sources

http://neptune.netimages.com/~chile/catalogs.html#sw

Cross Country Nurseries. A great source to buy mail-order chile plants and fantastic pictures of chiles!

http://www.chileplants.com

Simple Cooking Site. A great source of book reviews and comments about chiles.

http://www.outlawcook.com/

Cookbooks listed on the neptune site for southwestern sources

http://neptune.netimages.com/~chile/cookbooks.html

Links to many other chile related sites. The emphasis is on burning hot stuff .

http://www.ebicom.net/~howle/page/hotlinkn.htm

Although this is not about chiles, it does talk about Mezcal, which will make you feel very good while you're cooking. Great for Oaxaca nuts

http://www.mezcal.com/

Another excellent site with links to almost everywhere.

http://www.firegirl.com/

Need some cooking tips— check the following site which provides links to several great cooks.

http://www.firegirl.com/cooking/recipepointers.html

The following site has a long, long list of recipes. Like many things on the Web, you aren't really sure if these are the real things or just a mishmash of good and bad facts. However, check it out.

http://www.panix.com/~clay/cookbook/salsa.html

Mexican Dishes. Want to know about tortillas and moles, then check this out.

http://www.mexweb.com/food.htm

Purchase Santa Cruz Chili Products.

http://www.sunlandimports.com/foods.htm

OTHER TIDBITS OF INFORMATION

A Few Places to buy products:

You should always check for a local Latino market. Many of the chiles we mentioned are imported by these small merchants. Otherwise, a mail order company will be glad to sell you their products. The internet is a great place to locate the nearest mail order outlet and comparison shop.

National Spices, Jesse Martinez Food Inc.,
11410 North Cave Creek Road, Phoenix, Arizona 85020. Telephone: 602-997-5451

Santa Cruz Chili and Spice Company,
P. O. Box 177, Tumacacori, Arizona 85640. Telephone: 520-398-2591

Frieda's Inc,
P.O. Box 58488, L.A., Ca. 90058. Telephone: 800-241-9477

Native Seed Search :
526 N. 4th Avenue, Tucson, AZ 85705 , Telephone: (520)-622-5591 fax: 520-622-5591 email: jhosofaz@aol.com

Native Seeds Search in Tucson, Arizona collects wild chiltepin plants from the desert. They are very popular with home gardeners in the Tucson area. ***Chiltepin*** *grow in a dry region of Sonora known as Baviacora. The small vegetable gardens in which they grow are called huertas.*

combinations can be purchased as moist mixtures or soft cubes. Liquid is added to make a broth for cooking. Some dried chiles, especially chipotles (smoked jalapeños) are cooked and packed in a liquefied adobo mixture.

RECADOS: These are also mixtures of dried crushed chiles, spices and a tad of liquid. Recados are from the Yucatan and Tabasco region of Mexico and commonly use bitter Seville oranges (naranja agria) as moistening agents. They usually include cinnamon and achiote (crushed annato nut).

EN ESCABECHE: When chiles are canned, they are packed in vinegar. Chiles en escabeche are 'pickled' chiles.

MORE THAN A RELISH

We are amazed at the innumerable ways salsas are used in Mexico. Not only are they an ever present condiment they are often the primary ingredient in a dish. Although chiles can be used in very complex recipes, they are at their best in simple dishes.

One example would be **chilaquiles** (which means little chilied bits)– a delicious concoction of stale corn tortillas, deep fried, cut up, cooked with salsa and served with a cheese and cream topping. For extra substance chicken is sometimes added. There are endless versions of this dish depending on the sauce used.

Scrambled, fried or poached eggs are much more interesting when served with a variety of different salsas. One of our favorite Mexican breakfasts, **El Norteño**, consists of eggs scrambled with machaca or chorizo and then immersed in a picante ranchero sauce. It's served with refried beans and flour tortillas. And then there's **Huevos Tarascos**– a veritable medley of flavours. Begin with a corn tortilla, layer beans, cheese, a slice of cooked ham and then 2 eggs sunny side up. Drown the whole thing in a chile verde salsa. Or how about **Huevos Socorridos**– an omelet topped with a tomato and chile salsa and sprinkled with bacon bits, served with hot corn tortillas. And of course everybody is familiar with **Huevos Rancheros,** fried eggs on top of tortillas and beans and topped with a red ranchero salsa.

Salsas can add extra flavour and spice to simple appetizers. Whip up some cream cheese with a little milk and pico de gallo. Or, for a quick guacamole combine mashed avocado with Salsa Mexicana (see page 33). Heat your favorite meatballs in a chipotle salsa. Layer corn tortillas with your favorite salsa and cheese and heat in the oven. Or just serve a selection with the traditional dippers– vegetables, crackers, chips.

As a main course addition, salsa is a perfect compliment to fish or meat. Chipotles are particularly good added to mashed potatoes and corn blends nicely with any salsa. Salsas or chopped chiles can also be added to sandwiches.

As a condiment the possibilities are endless. Salsas are great with sandwiches and soups. They're a tasty low fat substitute for butter on potatoes and other vegetables. And, they add a world of flavour to salads– without the fat.

Index

A

B

C

D

E

F

G

H

J

M

N

O

P

We hope you enjoyed this book. We would love to hear your comments and suggestions. Please write to us at

Tiengui del Norte Publishing,

Box 62, 9920 - 63 Avenue

Edmonton, Alberta T6E 0G9

Canada

or email us at

rrrico@globalserve.net